HAMLET

By WILLIAM SHAKESPEARE

Preface and Annotations by
HENRY N. HUDSON

Introduction by
CHARLES HAROLD HERFORD

Hamlet
By William Shakespeare
Preface and Annotations by Henry N. Hudson
Introduction by Charles Harold Herford

Print ISBN 13: 978-1-4209-5214-8
eBook ISBN 13: 978-1-4209-5215-5

Cover Image: Ophelia (w/c on paper), Millais, Sir John Everett (1829-96) / Private Collection / Photo © Peter Nahum at The Leicester Galleries, London / Bridgeman Images.

Please visit *www.digireads.com*

CONTENTS

Preface

HAMLET, PRINCE OF DENMARK.

Registered at the Stationers' on the 26th of July, 1602, as "The Revenge of Hamlet, Prince of Denmark, as it was lately acted by the Lord Chamberlain's Servants." The tragedy was printed in 1603. It was printed again in 1604; and in the title-page of that issue we have the words, "enlarged to almost as much again as it was." This latter edition was reprinted in 1605, and again in 1611; besides an undated quarto, which is commonly referred to 1607, as it was entered at the Stationers' in the Fall of that year. These are all the issues known to have been made before the play reappeared in the folio of 1623. The quartos, all but the first, have a number of highly important passages that are not in the folio; while, on the other hand, the folio has a few, less important, that are wanting in the quartos.

It is generally agreed that the first issue was piratical. It gives the play but about half as long as the later quartos, and carries in its face abundant evidence of having been greatly marred and disfigured in the making-up. Dyce says, "It seems certain that in the quarto of 1603 we have Shakespeare's first conception of the play, though with a text mangled and corrupted throughout, and perhaps formed on the notes of some short-hand writer, who had imperfectly taken it down during representation." Nevertheless it is evident that the play was very different then from what it afterwards became. Polonius is there called Corambis, and his man Reynaldo is called Montano. Divers scenes and passages, some of them such as a reporter would be least likely to omit, are wanting altogether. The Queen is represented as concerting and actively co-operating with Hamlet against the King's life; and she has an interview of considerable length with Horatio, who informs her of Hamlet's escape from the ship bound for England, and of his safe return to Denmark; of which scene the later issues have no traces whatever. All this fully ascertains the play to have undergone a thorough recasting from what it was when the copy of 1603 was taken.

A good deal of question has been made as to the time when the tragedy was first written. It is all but certain that the subject was done into a play some years before Shakespeare took it in hand, as we have notices to that effect reaching as far back as 1589. That play, however, is lost; and our notices of it give no clue to the authorship. On the other hand, there appears no good reason for believing that any form of Shakespeare's *Hamlet* was in being long before we hear of it as entered at the Stationers', in 1602.

Whether, or how far, Shakespeare may have borrowed his materials from any pre-existing play on the subject, we have no means of knowing. The tragedy was partly founded on a work by Saxo Grammaticus, a Danish historian, written as early as 1204, but not printed till 1514. The incidents, as related by him, were borrowed by Belleforest, through whose French version, probably, the tale found its way to the English stage. It was called *The History of Hamblet*. As there told, the story is, both in matter and style, uncouth and barbarous in the last degree; a savage, shocking tale of lust and murder, unredeemed by a single touch of art or fancy in the narrator. The scene of the incidents is laid before the introduction of Christianity into Denmark, and when the Danish power held sway in England: further than this the time is not specified. A close sketch of such parts of the tale as were specially drawn upon for the play is all I have room for.

Roderick, King of Denmark, divided his kingdom into provinces, and placed governors in them. Among these were two warlike brothers, Horvendile and Fengon. The greatest honour that men of noble birth could at that time win was by piracy, wherein Horvendile surpassed all others. Collere, King of Norway, was so moved by his fame that he challenged him to fight, body to body; and the challenge was accepted, the victor to have all the riches that were in the other's ship. Collere was slain; and Horvendile returned home with much treasure, most of which he sent to King Roderick, who thereupon gave him his daughter Geruth in marriage. Of this marriage sprang Hamblet, the hero of the tale.

Fengon became so envious of his brother, that he resolved to kill him. Before doing this, he corrupted his wife, whom he afterwards married. Young Hamblet, thinking he was likely to fare no better than his father, went to feigning himself mad. One of Fengon's friends, suspecting his madness to be feigned, counselled Fengon to use some crafty means for discovering his purpose. The plot being all laid, the counsellor went into the Queen's chamber, and hid behind the hangings. Soon after, the Queen and the Prince came in; but the latter, suspecting some treachery, kept up his counterfeit of madness, and went to beating with his arms upon the hangings. Feeling something stir under them, he cried, "A rat, a rat!" and thrust his sword into them; which done, he pulled the man out half dead, and made an end of him. He then has a long interview with his mother, which ends in a pledge of mutual confidence between them. She engages to keep his secret faithfully, and to aid him in his purpose of revenge; swearing that she had often prevented his death, and that she had never consented to the murder of his father.

Fengon's next device was to send the Prince to England, with secret letters to have him there put to death. Two of his Ministers being sent along with him, the Prince, again suspecting mischief, when they were at sea read their commission while they were asleep, and substituted one requiring the bearers to be hanged. All this and much more being done, he returned to Denmark, and there executed his revenge in a manner horrid enough.

There is, besides, an episodical passage in the tale, from which the Poet probably took some hints, especially in the hero's melancholy mood, and his apprehension that "the spirit he has seen may be the Devil." I condense a portion of it: "In those days the northern parts of the world, living then under Satan's laws, were full of enchanters, so that there was not any young gentleman that knew not something therein. And so Hamblet had been instructed in that devilish art whereby the wicked spirit abuseth mankind. It toucheth not the matter herein to discover the parts of divination in man, and whether this Prince, by reason of his over-great melancholy, had received those impressions, divining that which never any had before declared." The "impressions" here spoken of refer to the means whereby Hamblet found out the secret of his father's murder.

It is hardly needful to add that Shakespeare makes the persons Christians, clothing them with the sentiments and manners of a much later period than they have in the tale; though he still places the scene at a time when England paid some sort of homage to the Danish crown; which was before the Norman Conquest. Therewithal the Poet uses very great freedom in regard to time; transferring to Denmark, in fact, the social and intellectual England of his own day.

We have seen that the *Hamlet* of 1604 was greatly enlarged. The enlargement, however, is mainly in the contemplative and imaginative parts, little being added in the way of action and incident. And in respect of those parts, there is no comparison between the two copies; the difference is literally immense. In the earlier text we have little more than a naked though in the main well-ordered and well-knit skeleton, which, in the later, is everywhere replenished and glorified with large, rich volumes of thought and poetry; where all that is incidental and circumstantial is made subordinate to the living energies of mind and soul.

HENRY N. HUDSON

Introduction

Hamlet, the longest of Shakespeare's plays, was never printed, as it was certainly never performed, entire, in his own time. Our authentic text is derived from two early versions, each defective in certain points: viz. the Quarto of 1604 (Q₂), and the Folio of 1623. The title-page of the Quarto runs:—

THE | Tragicall Historie of | HAMLET, | *Prince of Denmarke.* | By William Shakespeare. | Newly imprinted and enlarged to almost as much | againe as it was, according to the true and perfect | Coppie. | AT LONDON, | Printed by I. R. for N. L., and are to be sold at his | shoppe under Saint Dunstons Church in I Fleet Street. 1604.

This is the more valuable of the two editions, and the *Hamlet* texts of the last generation have steadily approximated towards it. But the Folio of 1623 was printed from an independent MS. containing some new passages as well as dropping many old; and while its variations in phrase were rarely for the better, it was much more accurately printed.

Four Quartos followed that of 1604, each printed substantially from its immediate predecessor in 1605, 1611, *circa* 1611-1637, and 1637.

In addition to these authentic editions of the Shakespearean text, two rude versions of the *Hamlet* story exist, which stand in a close but enigmatic relation to it. The so-called 'First Quarto' of *Hamlet* was unknown until 1821, when Sir Henry Bunbury discovered a copy bound up with nine other old Shakespearean Quartos.[1] Its title-page runs:—

THE | Tragicall Historie of | HAMLET | *Prince of Denmarke* | By William Shake-speare. | As it hath been diverse times acted by his Highnesse ser-|uants in the Cittie of London: as also in the two V-|niversities of Cambridge and Oxford, and else-where. At London printed for N. L. and John Trundell. 1603.[2]

---

[1] It is now in the library of the Duke of Devonshire. In 1856 a needy student raised a shilling on a second copy, now in the British Museum. The two copies supplement each other, the first lacking the last page, the second the title-page. Facsimiles have been published by Timmins, Ashbee, and Griggs.

[2] Thus the text is little more than half as long as the Second Quarto text—2143 lines to 3719; a large part of this must be laid to the account of omission and mutilation. What havoc this wrought may be judged from such *disjecta* membra as the following:—

All critics agree that this 'First Quarto' was a pirated edition, surreptitiously put together from notes taken in the theatre. The great majority agree that the original, which it thus rudely reproduced, was not the very *Hamlet* printed 'according to the true and perfect copy' in the Second Quarto, but an earlier version of the story, which underwent a revision by Shakespeare before it became the definitive *Hamlet* we know.[3]

In this earlier version itself, however, there is unmistakable evidence of Shakespeare's hand. Some of the profoundest things in *Hamlet* are absent; but many of his most pregnant and searching sayings are discernible, through a veil. On the other hand there are marks of altogether alien work.

Still more difficulty surrounds the German version of *Hamlet*, obtusely entitled, *Der bestrafte Brudermord.* It was first printed in 1781, from a MS. dated October 27, 1710. The language of the MS. is of the later seventeenth century, but the play itself undoubtedly belonged to the repertory of one or other of the bands of English players who entertained the courts and the cities of Germany from 1585 till far on into the war time, with their gross travesties of the masterpieces of the English stage. A good deal of Shakespearean poetry flashes amongst the wreckage of the First Quarto: here every ray is lost in an unbroken opacity of the vulgarest prose. It is possible, nevertheless, to see that the traducer operated upon a version of *Hamlet* identical neither with the First nor with the Second Quarto, but containing marks of both,—most probably the original text which the First Quarto attempted to reproduce.[4] The remarkable 'Prologus' in which 'Night' holds colloquy with the three Furies, and fires them on to vengeance upon the guilty king, has no known English original, but

---

> O my lord, the young Ofelia
> Having made a garland of sundrie sortes of floures,
> Sitting upon a willow by a brooke,
> The enuious sprig broke, into the brooke she fell,
> And for a while her clothes spread wide abroade
> Bore the young Lady up: and there she sat smiling
> Even mermaid-like, 'twixt heaven and earth, etc.
>
> (Sc. xv.)

[3] The most decisive points of the evidence are: (1) the *divergent names*. For Polonius and Reynaldo we find in Q₁ Corambis and Montano; (2) an entire scene (xiv.) not found in Q₂; (3) the queen is somewhat differently conceived, and has a somewhat different role. She solemnly protests her innocence of the murder, and joins with Horatio (in the scene referred to) and with Hamlet himself in plotting the revenge. In Q2 she is more unequivocally 'frail': her guilt, though not established, is hinted, and while she sympathises with Hamlet she is far too helpless to conspire. Many other slighter differences may be passed by.

[4] Corambus (Creizenach, *Die Schauspiele der engl. Comödianten*, p. 134).

points, like much of the First Quarto text, to a pre-Shakespearean version of the *Hamlet* story.

Of all the vanished plays of Elizabeth's time, the old or 'original' *Hamlet* is the most regrettable. A chorus of testimonies, from 1589 onwards, leave no doubt that there was such a play, but tell us little about it. The *locus classicus* is Nash's epistle prefixed to Greene's *Menaphon*, where he 'talks a little in friendship with a few of our triviall translators' to the following effect:—

'It is a common practice now-a-daies amongst a sort of shifting companions, that runne through every arte and thrive by none, to leave the trade of *Noverint* whereto they were borne, and busie themselves with the indevors of art, that could scarcelie latinize their necke-verse if they should have neede; yet English Seneca read by candle-light yeeldes manie good sentences, as *Bloud is a begger*, and so forth: and if you intreate him faire in a frostie morning, he will afoord you whole *Hamlets*, I should say handfulls, of tragical speaches. But O grief! *Tempus edax rerum;*—what's that will last alwaies? The sea exhaled by drops will in continuance be drie; and Seneca, let bloud line by line, and page by page, at length must needs die to our stage: which makes his famisht followers to imitate the Kidde in *Æsop*, .who enamored with the Foxes newfangles, forsooke all hopes of life to leape into a new occupation, and these men renouncing all possibilities of credit or estimation, to intermeddle with Italian translations,' etc.

The *Hamlet* thus in existence before 1590 was repeatedly played between 1590 and 1600;[5] and the melodramatic catchword, 'Hamlet, Revenge,' clung to the popular memory for years after it had been superseded in Shakespeare's *Hamlet*.[6] Even the entry of Shakespeare's play in the Stationers' Register, July 26, 1602, 'a booke called the Revenge of Hamlett,' probably betrays the dominance of the old version and the conception of the action which it had ingrained.

These meagre data make it probable that the old *Hamlet* was a tragedy of vengeance, strongly tinged with Senecan rhetoric, and set in motion, like Seneca's *Thyestes* and *Agamemnon*, by the appeal of the wronged man's ghost to his kin. Nash's acrid innuendoes, further, leave little doubt that the author was Thomas Kyd, on whose name, like Jonson, he condescends to pun. Kyd's father apparently belonged to the 'trade of Noverint,' and his *Spanish Tragedy* betrays just that 'prentice

---

[5] Henslowe records in his Diary under June 9, 1594, 'Rd. at hamlet, viijs.' He does not mark it as a new play. Lodge in his *Wits' Misery* (1596) records a trait of this or a later performance: '[Hate Virtue is] a foul lubber, and looks as pale as the wisard of the ghost, which cried so miserably at the theator, like an oyster-wife, *Hamlet revenge.*'

[6] 'My name's Hamlet revenge,' says Captain Tucca in Dekker's *Satiromastix*, 'thou hast been at Paris garden, hast not? (1602). The phrase is played upon also in *Westward Hoe* (1607), and Rowland's *Night Raven* (1618).

knowledge of Seneca which Nash brands in the old *Hamlet*.[7] There are speeches stuffed with Senecan reminiscences, and the whole action unfolds itself at the bidding of a ghost. But the play is in no sense antique: Elizabethan love of bustling action runs riot in the crowded plot. The chorus, the sentiments, and the messengers' reports are but classic embroidery somewhat incongruously pieced on to a garment of English homespun by a playwright who read his Seneca in English and 'by candle-light.'[8] *The Spanish Tragedy* had, then, unmistakable affinities with the old *Hamlet*, and enables us to conjecture with tolerable clearness the shape which the legendary tale of *Hamlet* took in his hands.

Even as told by Saxo, in the earliest extant version, the legend of *Hamlet* probably owes something to the genius of Rome. Saxo Grammaticus (i.e. 'the Lettered'), perhaps the most brilliant Latinist of the twelfth century, wrote his *History of the Danes* in evident emulation of the sumptuous and sonorous manner of Livy.[9] In what precise form he found the legend we cannot tell; but in his pages Amlothi, the sea-giant who looms vaguely in a phrase of the Edda, tossing the white beach-pebbles like meal from his 'mill,' has become a Northern counterpart of the Livian Brutus who expelled the Tarquins. Like Brutus he feigns madness or 'folly' to save his life, and his feigning is the mainspring of the whole intrigue.[10] The usurper Feng (*Claudius*), whose crimes are told at length, tries to entrap him into confession by a series of devices. A girl is thrown in his way; a crafty old counsellor listens unseen to his talk with his mother; finally he is sent to England with two guards and secret orders for his death. Amleth's craft everywhere triumphs: he keeps the saving veil of eccentricity before the maiden, kills the eavesdropping counsellor, and provides for his two guards the death to which they were leading him. After winning the daughter of the king of England he returns, slays the tyrant, justifies his deed in an oration to the assembled people, and is chosen king. He is no sooner crowned than he has to cope with the machinations of his father-

---

[7] The phrase 'Bloud is a beggar,' which Nash quotes from the old *Hamlet*, has a parallel in a sentence from a tract of Kyd's: 'Bloud is an inceasant crier in the eares of the Lord. Sarrazin, *Anglia*, xiii. 124. Armin's 'There are, as Hamlet says, things called whips in store' (*Nest of Ninnies*, 1608), may rest upon a confusion with *The Spanish Tragedy*, where this often-parodied phrase occurs, but at least shows that the two plays were classed together.

[8] Cf. R. Fischer, *Zur Kunstentwicklung der engl. Tragödie*, p. 94 f.

[9] Cf. Mr. O. Elton's valuable Appendix to his translation of the First Nine Books of Saxo.

[10] As is well known, the 'simpleton' Amleth took root in the Scandinavian mind and languages. 'The king clapped his hands together and laughed, just as if he were an Amblode,' *den intet god forstode*, runs an old Swedish rhyme quoted by Vigfusson, *s.v.* 'amlóð.'

in-law, and marries a second wife, the 'Amazon' Hermentrude, by whose treachery he himself finally falls.

Out of this rambling *History of Hamlet* the old playwright made his Tragedy of Revenge by a process somewhat as follows. He added the ghost, whose summons spurs Hamlet to the revenge which Saxo's Amleth conceives unaided. The ghost probably told the story of his own death, which, in a play like *King Leir*, would have been visibly set forth. The tragedy certainly ended with the accomplishment of vengeance, and Hamlet, like Hieronymo, shared his victim's doom. It was assuredly not reserved to Shakespeare to silence the superfluous sequel. Moreover, if the summons to revenge opened the play and the act of revenge closed it, Hamlet necessarily 'delayed'; and the example of Hieronymo suggests that he already cried out at his own tardiness, already saw the phantom of the dead chiding his 'lapse in time and passion,'[11] was already stung with shame to see others do (like the Player and Fortinbras) what he neglects:—

> See, see, O see thy shame, Hieronymo!
> See here a loving father to his son. . . .

Hieronymo entraps his victims by a play, and the earlier Hamlet probably used a device familiar long before Shakespeare, to catch the conscience of the king.[12]

In 1585-86 English players performed in the Kronborg at Helsingör. It is probable that their impressions and reports were already

---

[11] Hieronymo in his wildness takes the old man, who has also lost a son, for his dead Horatio and bursts out:—

> Art thou not come, Horatio, from the depth
> To ask for justice in this upper earth,
> To tell thy father thou art unreveng'd . . .
> To plague Hieronymo that is remiss,
> And seeks not vengeance for Horatio's death?

We are brought very near Hamlet's conscience-stricken cry:—

> Do you not come your tardy son to chide? . . .

[12] It is plausibly suggested that the idea originated in the well-known anecdote in the *Warning for Fair Women*, and glanced at in *Hamlet* (ii, 2. 617), of the woman at Lynn who had murdered her husband:—

> And sitting to behold a tragedy . . .
> Wherein a woman that had murthered hers
> Was ever haunted with her husband's ghost
> She was so moved with the sight thereof
> As she cried out the play was made by her [about her],
> And openly confess her husband's murder.

reflected in the old *Hamlet;* that Saxo's Juteland had already become Shakespeare's Elsinore; that Hamlet's attendants were already called Rosencrantz and Guildenstern.[13]

Finally, there is a good deal of evidence for holding that the old *Hamlet,* like *The Spanish Tragedy* and *Solimon and Perseda,* opened with a symbolical dialogue between the supernatural contrivers of the harms,—the original, in fact, of that remarkable 'Prologus' of the *Bestrafte Brudermord.* The brief, fierce debate between Hecate and the Furies is foreshadowed in the dumb show of *Gorbodric* (Act IV.), .where the Furies, 'daughters of the night,' move with their whips and snakes across the stage. No classical *motif* died harder in English tragedy; but for it, probably, the weird sisters themselves would have looked less like Furies than they do, and been less closely allied to Hecate.[14] Of the action of the play the Prologue says little, but its allusive hints fall in with our other indications of the pre-Shakespearean drama. The king's incestuous marriage is to be punished with discord. 'Mingle poison in their spousal and jealousy in their hearts!' cries Hecate. Such a queen naturally became the secret ally of the avenger, like Bell' Imperia in *The Spanish Tragedy,* and this conception of Gertrude still lingers, as we have seen in the First Quarto, when she vows complicity with Hamlet:—

> I will conceale, consent and doe my best,
> What stratagem soe'er thou shalt devise.

She echoes the very phrases of Bell' Imperia:—

> Hieronymo, I will consent, conceale; ...
> *Hier.* On then, whatsoever I devise
> Let me entreat you, grace my practices.

It is hard to resist the evidence of such passages that in the earliest version of *Hamlet* fragments at least of the lost *Hamlet* remain embedded.[15] Probably the whole of the scene between the queen and Horatio (xi.) omitted in the final versions is such a fragment.[16]

---

[13] ii. 1077-1087.

[14] Sarrazin (*Anglia,* xiii. 121) thinks that these scenes in *Macbeth* were influenced by the original of the Prologue itself.

[15] This view has been urged with great force and learning by Sarrazin in the article already quoted (*Anglia,* xiii. 117 f.).

[16] Such a fragment too is the king's sentiment in Q₁ (Sc. ii. 4, 7):—

> None lives on earth but hee is borne to die,
> almost an echo of Kyd's version of Garnier's *Cornélie:*—
> And whatsoever lives is sure to die.
>
> (Hazl. *Dodsl.* v. 199.)

We may conclude then that the old play already presented the rough-hewn framework of the action of *Hamlet*, with hints of Ophelia and Polonius, perhaps of Rosencrantz and Guildenstern, and some pregnant suggestions of Hamlet himself. If *Hamlet* is the most individual of all Shakespeare's works, if it is penetrated with the personal accent beyond any other dramatic utterance of man, it probably owes even less than usual—less certainly than *Macbeth* or *Lear*—to inventive construction of plot. But Shakespeare's supreme power of wholly transforming the spiritual complexion of a tale while leaving its material form almost intact, is nowhere so wonderfully seen.

The spiritual complexion of the Shakespearean *Hamlet* is, in its last nuances, beyond analysis. Its far-reaching affinities with the mind of other times are charged with the most vivid suggestions of its own; its universality is full of local colour; its local colour penetrated with ideal gleams.

Outer evidence points clearly to 1601 as the date of the text imperfectly represented in the First Quarto. On July 26, 1602, this text was entered in the Stationers' Register. The allusions in this text to the 'travelling' of the players and to its cause, correspond to the known situation of Shakespeare's own company during the previous year. We know that they 'travelled' towards the end of the year, playing, among other places, at Cambridge, and performing, among other pieces, the newly-finished *Hamlet*,—which the edition of 1603 announced as having been diverse times acted by the Company in the two Universities. We know also that, before they travelled, the Children of the Chapel on the private stages had become formidable competitors of the public stage. And it would seem that this competition must have become formidable to the Globe Company later than September 29, 1600, when Burbage, its manager, leased the Blackfriars Theatre to Evans, the *régisseur* of the Children.[17]

In the authentic 1604 Quarto the sarcastic description of the Children is cut out, and the travelling ascribed vaguely to a late 'innovation.' The fact that Shakespeare's fellow-actors printed both versions together in the Folio goes to show that the second is only a more formal reference to the same circumstance as the first.

To trace any inner connexion between *Hamlet* and Shakespeare's history is less easy. Nothing that we know of Shakespeare's personal history really explains the startling and sudden intensity of personal accent in *Hamlet*, or the changed outlook upon the world which here first becomes apparent. His father's death in 1601, the execution of Essex and imprisonment of Southampton early in the same year, may

---

Shakespeare transferred this 'vacant chaff, well meant for grain,' to his queen, whose ambiguous neutrality it aptly conveyed.

[17] Cf. W. Hall Griffin, *Hamlet*, p. xxi.

have lent fervour to Hamlet's outbursts of grief and of friendship. Montaigne's *Essays*, in Florio's excellent English, may have contributed to the speculative subtlety of his speech. But these things carry us little way towards explaining *Hamlet.* A deep inward convulsion is no doubt revealed in the *Sonnets.* But we are not at liberty to see in the world-weariness of Hamlet a direct reflexion of the 'hell of time'[18] which Shakespeare suffered from his branded name and his friend estranged, or to hear the echo of Shakespeare's cry for restful death[19] in Hamlet's 'To be, or not to be.' The evidence rather tends to show that when Shakespeare unlocked his heart in these bitter verses his imagination was bodying forth the joyous comedy of Falstaff or Fluellen. What is clear is that Shakespeare had himself lived through all the desolation that he makes Hamlet express; but it is when experience has subsided into a vibrating memory that it becomes stuff for drama. And *Hamlet* is not the only reflexion of this mood. From about 1600 to 1604 Shakespeare shows a disposition to draw, with a peculiar acerbity, pictures of corrupt cities and courts, and with a peculiar sympathy, always touched with irony, the thinking and feeling men whom the spectacle of such societies turns into cynics or satirists, plunges into despondence or goads to reform. Jaques pierces the body of court and city with shafts of choice invective, discharged with curious and self-conscious art. The duke in *Measure for Measure* is bent upon healing his plague-stricken city, but has not the nerve to apply the cauterising iron. Brutus, with sterner resolve but less insight, heroically strikes the blow and perishes amidst the ruin he has wrought. It is not difficult to imagine how the elements of ineffectual idealism here detached may have gathered in Shakespeare's mind about the character of the Danish prince, who even in the Saga had loitered towards his deed of death, and loved his motley somewhat too well. Transferred to a modern society, as polished on the surface as Brutus' Rome, and as corrupt at the core as the duke's Vienna, new possibilities opened for the legend of the tardy avenger. A brain solely occupied with the business of avenging a particular crime becomes a highly-strung organism acutely sensitive to every harmony of civil refinement, and every jar of moral discord. He sees his personal wrongs on a background of general corruption. Everything in *Hamlet* converges upon Hamlet, and his complex animosity to evil is thrown into relief by the elementary vindictiveness of his antitypes Fortinbras and Laertes,—Shakespeare's own extraordinarily effective additions to the legend. Fortinbras is not without a trace of Hamlet's nobleness, or Laertes of his accomplishment. But neither has any thought save of personal vengeance. Hamlet's shafts of invective glance aside from the king to

---

[18] *Sonnet* cxxiv.
[19] *Sonnet* lxvi.

the whole society of which the king is the type. He brings that society to the bar of an idealism as lofty and noble as Brutus', and riddles its pretensions with a poignancy which Jaques cannot approach. His dream of the greatness of man—'infinite in faculty, in action like an angel, in apprehension like a god'—is a Humanist counterpart of the austere Stoic sense of human dignity which nerves the dagger of Brutus against the supposed tyranny of Caesar. And all the brilliant culture of Humanism, which we rather presume than recognise in Jaques,—its wit, its various dexterity, its delight in the stage,—are mirrored in his incomparably vivid speech. But his intellect and passion are mysteriously involved in his doom. Brutus' abstract faith in man carries him resolutely to ruin without suffering disillusion; Hamlet's bitter penetration shatters the very bases of that exalted dream, and disillusion paralyses resolve. If he sees the world as an unweeded garden, it is because he alone has eyes for the fretted canopy of heaven. But amid all his pessimism, 'art still has truth'; man is a 'quintessence of dust,' but the next moment he is giving a genial welcome to the strolling players, somewhat as Jaques forgets his melancholy in the delightful discovery of Touchstone. It is not for nothing that he is made the mouthpiece of Shakespeare's ripest convictions about the art of playing; for he wears his own disguise with something of the player's zest, and is allured away from his purpose by the intellectual fascination of his role.

The Brutus and the Jaques types are as it were promontories in the sea of Hamlet: promontories which, if not 'sterile,' yet do not carry us within sight of shore. A mysterious residuum always remains, and the history of the attempts to solve it approaches in intellectual fascination, and exceeds in intellectual value, the task of solution itself. Three generations have seen their own philosophic and racial idiosyncrasies in the elusive mirror of Hamlet. To the humanity of Goethe he was a pure and lovely nature; to the speculative idealism of Coleridge the problem lay in his over-reflecting intellect; to the Hegelian religiosity of Ulrici, in his tender conscience; to Schopenhauer, in his world-weariness. With the reaction from the philosophies of pure thought and from the old Germany of pure thinkers, new Hamlets have arisen, whose difficulties lie in their 'spleen' (Hermann Grimm), their 'temperament' (Gessner), or their 'sluggish blood' (Loening); or in the restraints imposed by external sanctions of law and politics. If modern psychology lives in Loening's 'lazy Hamlet,' the political Teuton of to-day is reflected in Werder's scornful 'dismissal' of the dreamer Hamlet to limbo in company with the dreaming Germany of which Freytag proclaimed him the type. Finally, to the 'realistic' eyes of our time

Hamlet has become a veiled allusion, and his spiritual profile an ineffectual disguise, for Essex,[20] Montaigne, or James the First.

CHARLES HAROLD HERFORD

1904.

---

[20] This is the contention of Hermann Conrad in a series of elaborate articles recently reprinted in his *Shakspere's Selbstbekenntnisse*, 1897.

The Tragedy of Hamlet, Prince of Denmark

DRAMATIS PERSONAE

CLAUDIUS, *King of Denmark*
HAMLET, *son to the former and nephew to the present King*
POLONIUS, *Lord Chamberlain*
HORATIO, *friend to Hamlet*
LAERTES, *son to Polonius*
VOLTEMAND, CORNELIUS, ROSENCRANTZ,
    GUILDENSTERN, OSRIC, *Gentleman courtiers*
A Gentleman
A Priest
MARCELLUS, BERNARDO, *officers*
FRANCISCO, *a soldier*
REYNALDO, *servant to Polonius*
Players
Two Clowns, grave-diggers
FORTINBRAS, *Prince of Norway*
A Norwegian Captain
English Ambassadors
GERTRUDE, *Queen of Denmark, mother to Hamlet*
OPHELIA, *daughter to Polonius*
Ghost of Hamlet's Father
Lords, Ladies, Officers, Soldiers, Sailors, Messengers, and
    Attendants.

THE SCENE: DENMARK.

ACT I.

SCENE I.

Elsinore. A Platform before the Castle.

[FRANCISCO *at his post. Enter to him* BERNARDO.]

BERNARDO. Who's there?
FRANCISCO. Nay, answer me:[21] stand, and unfold yourself.
BERNARDO. Long live the king!
FRANCISCO. Bernardo?
BERNARDO. He.
FRANCISCO. You come most carefully upon your hour.
BERNARDO. 'Tis now struck twelve; get thee to bed, Francisco.
FRANCISCO. For this relief much thanks: 'tis bitter cold,
    And I am sick at heart.
BERNARDO. Have you had quiet guard?
FRANCISCO. Not a mouse stirring.
BERNARDO. Well, good night.
    If you do meet Horatio and Marcellus,
    The rivals[22] of my watch, bid them make haste.
FRANCISCO. I think I hear them. Stand, ho! Who's there?

[*Enter* HORATIO *and* MARCELLUS.]

HORATIO. Friends to this ground.
MARCELLUS. And liegemen to the Dane.
FRANCISCO. Give you good night.[23]
MARCELLUS. O, farewell, honest soldier:
    Who hath relieved you?
FRANCISCO. Bernardo has my place.
    Give you good night. [*Exit.*]
MARCELLUS. Holla! Bernardo!
BERNARDO. Say,
    What, is Horatio there?

---

[21] Answer *me*, as I have the right to challenge *you.* Bernardo then gives in answer the watchword, "Long live the King!"

[22] *Rivals* are associates or partners. A brook, rivulet, or river, *rivus*, being a natural boundary between different proprietors, was owned by them in common; that is, they were *partners* in the right and use of it. From the strifes thus engendered, the *partners* came to be *contenders*: hence the ordinary sense of *rival.*

[23] This salutation is an abbreviated form of, "May God give you a good night"; which has been still further abbreviated into, "Good night."

HORATIO A. piece of him.
BERNARDO. Welcome, Horatio: welcome, good Marcellus.
MARCELLUS. What, has this thing appear'd again to-night?[24]
BERNARDO. I have seen nothing.
MARCELLUS. Horatio says 'tis but our fantasy,
    And will not let belief take hold of him
    Touching this dreaded sight, twice seen of us:
    Therefore I have entreated him along
    With us to watch the minutes of this night;
    That if again this apparition come,
    He may approve our eyes[25] and speak to it.
HORATIO. Tush, tush, 'twill not appear.
BERNARDO. Sit down awhile;
    And let us once again assail your ears,
    That are so fortified against our story
    What[26] we have two nights seen.
HORATIO. Well, sit we down,
    And let us hear Bernardo speak of this.
BERNARDO. Last night of all,
    When yond same star that's westward from the pole[27]
    Had made his course[28] to illume that part of heaven
    Where now it burns, Marcellus and myself,
    The bell then beating one—
MARCELLUS. Peace, break thee off; look, where it comes again!

[*Enter the* GHOST.]

BERNARDO. In the same figure, like the king that's dead.
MARCELLUS. Thou art a scholar; speak to it, Horatio.[29]
BERNARDO. Looks it not like the king? mark it, Horatio.
HORATIO. Most like: it harrows[30] me with fear and wonder.

---

[24] There is a temperate scepticism, well befitting a scholar, in Horatio's "has this *thing* appeared again to-night." *Thing* is the most general and indefinite substantive in the language. Observe the gradual approach to what is more and more definite. "Dreaded sight" cuts off a large part of the indefiniteness, and "this apparition" is a further advance to the particular. The matter is aptly ordered for what Coleridge calls "*credibilizing* effect."

[25] That is, *make good* our vision, or *prove* our eyes to be *true. Approve* was often thus used in the sense of *confirm.*

[26] "*With an account of* what," is the meaning; the language is elliptical.

[27] Of course the *polar star*, or north star, is meant, which appears to stand still, while the other stars in its neighbourhood seem to revolve around it.

[28] *His* for *its*, as usual.

[29] It was believed that a supernatural being could only be spoken to with effect by persons of learning; exorcisms being usually practiced by the clergy in Latin. So in *The Night Walker* of Beaumont and Fletcher: "Let's call the butler up, for he speaks Latin, and that will daunt the Devil."

BERNARDO. It would be spoke to.[31]
MARCELLUS. Question it, Horatio.
HORATIO. What art thou that usurp'st this time of night,
    Together with that fair and warlike form
    In which the majesty of buried Denmark
    Did sometimes[32] march? by heaven I charge thee, speak!
MARCELLUS. It is offended.
BERNARDO. See, it stalks away!
HORATIO. Stay! speak, speak! I charge thee, speak!

[*Exit* GHOST.]

MARCELLUS. 'Tis gone, and will not answer.
BERNARDO. How now, Horatio! you tremble and look pale:
    Is not this something more than fantasy?
    What think you on't?
HORATIO. Before my God, I might not this believe
    Without the sensible and true avouch
    Of mine own eyes.
MARCELLUS. Is it not like the king?
HORATIO. As thou art to thyself:
    Such was the very armour he had on
    When he the ambitious Norway combated;
    So frown'd he once, when, in an angry parle,
    He smote the sledded Polacks[33] on the ice.
    'Tis strange.
MARCELLUS. Thus twice before, and jump[34] at this dead hour,
    With martial stalk hath he gone by our watch.
HORATIO. In what particular thought to work I know not;
    But in the gross and scope of my opinion,
    This bodes some strange eruption to our state.[35]
MARCELLUS. Good now,[36] sit down, and tell me, he that knows,

---

[30] To *harrow* is to *distress*, to *vex*, to *disturb*. To *harry* and to *harass* have the same origin. Milton has the word in *Comus*: "Amazed I stood *harrow d* with grief and fear."

[31] *Would* and *should* were often used indiscriminately. I am not clear, however, whether the meaning here is, "It *wants* to be spoke to," or "It *ought* to be spoke to." Perhaps both.

[32] *Sometimes* and *sometime* were used indiscriminately, and often, as here, in the sense of *formerly.*

[33] *Polacks* was used for *Polanders* in Shakespeare's time. *Sledded* is *sledged*; on a sled or *sleigh.—Parle* is the same as *parley.*

[34] *Jump* and *just* were synonymous in the Poet's time. So in Chapman's *May-day*, 1611: "Your appointment was *jumpe* at three with me."

[35] Horatio means that, in a general interpretation of the matter, this foreshadows some great evil or disaster to the State; though he cannot conceive in what particular shape the evil is to come.

[36] "*Good* now" was often used precisely as the phrase "*well* now." Also, *good for*

Why this same strict and most observant watch
So nightly toils the subject[37] of the land,
And why such daily cast of brazen cannon,
And foreign mart for implements of war;
Why such impress[38] of shipwrights, whose sore task
Does not divide the Sunday from the week;
What might be toward,[39] that this sweaty haste
Doth make the night joint-labourer with the day:
Who is't that can inform me?

HORATIO. That can I;
At least, the whisper goes so.[40] Our last king,
Whose image even but now appear'd to us,
Was, as you know, by Fortinbras of Norway,
Thereto prick'd on[41] by a most emulate pride,
Dared to the combat; in which our valiant Hamlet—
For so this side of our known world esteem'd him—
Did slay this Fortinbras; who by a seal'd compact,
Well ratified by law and heraldry,[42]
Did forfeit, with his life, all those his lands
Which he stood seized of,[43] to the conqueror:
Against the which, a moiety competent[44]
Was gaged by our king; which had return'd
To the inheritance of Fortinbras,
Had he been vanquisher; as, by the same co-mart,[45]
And carriage of the article design'd,[46]

---

well.
    [37] The Poet sometimes uses an adjective with the sense of the plural substantive; as here *subject* for *subjects.*—*Toils* is here a transitive verb.—*Mart*, in the next line but one, is *trade.*
    [38] *Impress* here means pressing or forcing of men into the service.—*Divide*, next line, is *distinguish.* Of course, *week* is put for *week-days.*
    [39] *Toward*, here, is *at hand*, or *forthcoming.* Often so used.
    [40] That is, "so as I am going to tell you."
    [41] *Prick'd on* refers to Fortinbras; the sense being, "by Fortinbras, *who was* prick'd on thereto."
    [42] "Law *and* heraldry" is the same as "*the* law *of* Heraldry"; what is sometimes called "the code of honour." Private duels were conducted "according to an established code, and heralds had full authority in the matter. The Poet has many like expressions. So in *The Merchant*, v. 1: "I was beset with shame *and* courtesy"; which means "with *the* shame of *discourtesy*" Also in *King Lear*, i. 2: "This policy *and reverence of* age makes the world bitter," &c.; "This policy, or *practice, of reverencing* age."
    [43] This is the old legal phrase, still in use, for *held possession of*, or *was the rightful owner of.*
    [44] *Moiety competent* is *equivalent portion.* The proper meaning of *moiety* is *half;* so that the sense here is, half of the entire value put in pledge on both sides.—*Gaged* is *pledged.*
    [45] *Co-mart* is *joint-bargain* or *mutual agreement;* the same as *compact* a little before. So, in the preceding speech, *mart* for *trade*, or *bargain.*
    [46] *Design'd* in the sense of the Latin *designatus; marked out* or *drawn up. Carriage*

His fell to Hamlet. Now, sir, young Fortinbras,
Of unimproved mettle[47] hot and full,
Hath in the skirts of Norway here and there
Shark'd up[48] a list of lawless resolutes,
For food and diet, to some enterprise
That hath a stomach in't;[49] which is no other,
As it doth well appear unto our state,
But to recover of us, by strong hand
And terms compulsatory, those foresaid lands
So by his father lost: and this, I take it,
Is the main motive of our preparations,
The source of this our watch and the chief head
Of this post-haste and romage[50] in the land.

BERNARDO. I think it be no other but e'en so:
Well may it sort[51] that this portentous figure
Comes armed through our watch; so like the king
That was and is the question of these wars.

HORATIO. A mote it is to trouble the mind's eye.
In the most high and palmy[52] state of Rome,
A little ere the mightiest Julius fell,
The graves stood tenantless and the sheeted dead
Did squeak and gibber in the Roman streets:
So,[53] stars with trains of fire and dews of blood,
Disasters in the sun; and the moist star,[54]
Upon whose influence Neptune's empire stands
Was sick almost to doomsday[55] with eclipse:

---

is *purport* or *drift*.

[47] *Mettle*, in Shakespeare, is *spirit, temper, disposition.—Unimproved* is commonly explained *unimpeached, unquestioned*; and so, it appears, the word was sometimes used. But it may here mean *rude, wild, uncultured*; since Fortinbras, as "like well to like," may well be supposed of a somewhat *lawless* spirit.

[48] *Skark'd up* is *snapped up*, or *raked together*; the idea being, that Fortinbras has gathered eagerly, wherever he could, a band of desperadoes, hard cases, or roughs, who were up to any thing bold and adventurous, and required no pay but their keep.

[49] *Stomach* was often used in the sense of *courage*, or appetite for danger or for fighting.

[50] *Romage*, now spelt *rummage*, is used for ransacking, or making a thorough search.

[51] *Sort*, probably, for *happen*, or *fallout*. Often so. The word was sometimes used for suit, *fit*, or *agree*, which *may be* the sense here.

[52] *Palmy* is *victorious*; the *palm* being the old badge of victory.

[53] *So* is here equivalent, apparently, to *in like sort*, or *like manner*, and naturally draws in the sense of *there were*; unless we choose to regard these words as understood.

[54] "The moist star" is the Moon; so called, no doubt, either from the dews that attend her shining, or from her connection with the tides.—"Disasters in the Sun," is astrological, referring to the calamities supposed to be portended by certain aspects or conditions of that luminary.

[55] *Doomsday* is the old word for *judgment-day*. The meaning is that the Moon was

And even the like precurse of fierce[56] events,
As harbingers preceding still the fates
And prologue to the omen[57] coming on,
Have heaven and earth together demonstrated
Unto our climature[58] and countrymen.
But soft, behold! lo, where it comes again!

[*Re-enter the* GHOST.]

I'll cross it, though it blast me.[59]—Stay, illusion!
If thou hast any sound, or use of voice,
Speak to me:
If there be any good thing to be done,
That may to thee do ease and grace to me,
Speak to me:
If thou art privy to thy country's fate,
Which, happily, foreknowing[60] may avoid,
O, speak!
Or if thou hast uphoarded in thy life
Extorted treasure in the womb of earth,
For which, they say, you spirits oft walk in death,
Speak of it: [*The cock crows.*]
       stay, and speak! Stop it, Marcellus.
MARCELLUS. Shall I strike at it with my partisan?[61]
HORATIO. Do, if it will not stand.
BERNARDO. 'Tis here!
HORATIO. 'Tis here!
MARCELLUS. 'Tis gone! [*Exit* GHOST.]
       We do it wrong, being so majestical,
       To offer it the show of violence;
       For it is, as the air, invulnerable,

---

sick almost unto death.

       [56] The Poet repeatedly uses *fierce* in the general sense of *violent, swift, excessive, vehement.* So he has "*fierce* vanities," "*fierce* abridgment," and "*fierce* wretchedness."—*Precurse* for *precursor, forerunner.*

       [57] *Omen* is here put for *portentous* or *ominous event.*

       [58] *Climature* for clime or *climate;* used in a local sense.

       [59] It was believed that a person crossing the path of a spectre became subject to its malignant influence. Lodge's *Illustrations of English History,* speaking of Ferdinand, Earl of Derby, has the following: "On Friday there appeared a tall man, *who twice crossed him* swiftly; and when the earl came to the place where he saw this man, he fell sick."

       [60] Which *happy* or *fortunate foreknowledge* may avoid, a participle and adverb used with the sense of a substantive and adjective.—It was an old *superstition* that, if a man had "devoured widows' houses" or the portion of orphans, he could not lie quiet in his grave.

       [61] *Partisan* was a *halbert or pike;* a weapon used by watchmen.

And our vain blows malicious mockery.

BERNARDO. It was about to speak, when the cock crew.

HORATIO. And then it started like a guilty thing
Upon a fearful summons. I have heard,
The cock, that is the trumpet to the morn,
Doth with his lofty and shrill-sounding throat
Awake the god of day; and, at his warning,
Whether in sea or fire, in earth or air,
The extravagant and erring[62] spirit hies
To his confine:[63] and of the truth herein
This present object made probation.[64]

MARCELLUS. It faded on the crowing of the cock.
Some say that ever 'gainst that season comes
Wherein our Saviour's birth is celebrated,
The bird of dawning singeth all night long:
And then, they say, no spirit dares stir abroad;
The nights are wholesome; then no planets strike,
No fairy takes,[65] nor witch hath power to charm,
So hallowed and so gracious is the time.

HORATIO. So have I heard and do in part believe it.
But, look, the morn, in russet mantle clad,
Walks o'er the dew of yon high eastward hill:[66]
Break we our watch up;[67] and by my advice,
Let us impart what we have seen to-night
Unto young Hamlet; for, upon my life,
This spirit, dumb to us, will speak to him.
Do you consent we shall acquaint him with it,

---

[62] *Extravagant* is *extra-vagans*, wandering about, going beyond bounds. *Erring* is *erraticus*, straying or roving up and down.

[63] *Confine* for *place of confinement.*—This is a very ancient belief. Prudentius has a hymn, *Ad Gallicinium*, which aptly illustrates the text:

Ferunt, vagantes Dæmonas,	Hoc esse signum præscii
Lætos tenebris Noctium,	Norunt repromisæ Spei,
Gallo canente exterritos	Qua nos soporis liberi
Sparsim timere, et cedere.	Speramus adventum Dei.

[64] *Probation* is *proof,* or the act of proving. Repeatedly so.

[65] *Take* was used for *blast, infect,* or *smite with disease.* So in *King Lear,* ii. 4: "Strike her young bones, you *taking* airs, with lameness."—*Gracious* sometimes means *full of grace* or of the *Divine favour.*

[66] These last three speeches are admirably conceived. The speakers are in a highly kindled state; when the Ghost vanishes, their terror presently subsides into an inspiration of the finest quality, and their intense excitement, as it passes off, blazes up in a subdued and pious rapture of poetry.

[67] This, let the grammarians say what they will, is a clear instance of the first person plural, in the imperative mood. The same has occurred once before: "Well, *sit we down,* and *let us hear* Bernardo speak of this."

As needful in our loves, fitting our duty?
MARCELLUS. Let's do't, I pray; and I this morning know
  Where we shall find him most conveniently. [*Exeunt.*]

SCENE II.

The Same. A Room in the Castle.

[*Flourish. Enter* CLAUDIUS, *the* KING *of Denmark*, GERTRUDE,
the QUEEN, *and Councillors, including* POLONIUS, *his son*
LAERTES, VOLTEMAND, CORNELIUS, *and* HAMLET.]

KING. Though yet of Hamlet our dear brother's death
  The memory be green, and that[68] it us befitted
  To bear our hearts in grief and our whole kingdom
  To be contracted in one brow of woe,
  Yet so far hath discretion fought with nature
  That we with wisest sorrow think on him,
  Together with remembrance of ourselves.
  Therefore our sometime[69] sister, now our queen,
  The imperial jointress[70] to this warlike state,
  Have we, as 'twere with a defeated joy,
  With an auspicious and a dropping eye,[71]
  With mirth in funeral and with dirge in marriage,
  In equal scale weighing delight and dole,
  Taken to wife: nor have we herein barr'd
  Your better wisdoms, which have freely gone
  With this affair along. For all, our thanks.[72]
    Now follows, that you know,[73] young Fortinbras,
  Holding a weak supposal of our worth,
  Or thinking by our late dear brother's death

---

[68] Instead *of that*, present usage would repeat *though*. But in such cases the old language in full was *though that, if that, since that, when that*, &c.; and Shakespeare, in a second clause, very often uses the latter word instead of repeating the first.

[69] *Sometime*, in the sense of *former* ox *formerly*.

[70] *Jointress* is the same as *heiress*. The Poet herein follows the history, which represents the former King to have come to the throne by marriage; so that whatever of hereditary claim Hamlet has to the crown is in right of his mother.

[71] The same thought occurs in *The Winter's Tale*, v. 2: "She had *one eye declined* for the loss of her husband, *another elevated* that the oracle was fulfill'd." There is an old proverbial phrase, "To laugh with one eye, and cry with the other."

[72] Note the strained, elaborate, and antithetic style of the King's speech thus far. As he is there shamming and playing the hypocrite, he naturally tries how finely he can word it. In what follows, he speaks like a man, his mind moving with simplicity and directness as soon as he comes to plain matters of business.

[73] "Now follows that *which*, you know *already*" *That* was continually used where we should use *what*.

Our state to be disjoint[74] and out of frame,
Colleaguèd[75] with the dream of his advantage,
He hath not fail'd to pester us with message,
Importing the surrender of those lands
Lost by his father, with all bands[76] of law,
To our most valiant brother. So much for him.
Now for ourself and for this time of meeting:
Thus much the business is: we have here writ
To Norway, uncle of young Fortinbras—
Who, impotent and bed-rid, scarcely hears
Of this his nephew's purpose—to suppress
His further gait herein; in that[77] the levies,
The lists and full proportions, are all made
Out of his subject: and we here dispatch
You, good Cornelius, and you, Voltemand,
For bearers of this greeting to old Norway;
Giving to you no further personal power
To[78] business with the king, more than the scope
Of these delated articles allow.[79]
Farewell, and let your haste commend your duty.

CORNELIUS VOLTEMAND. In that and all things will we show our
duty.

KING. We doubt it nothing: heartily farewell.

[*Exeunt* VOLTEMAND *and* CORNELIUS.]

And now, Laertes, what's the news with you?
You told us of some suit; what is't, Laertes?
You cannot speak of reason[80] to the Dane,
And loose your voice: what wouldst thou beg, Laertes,
That shall not be my offer, not thy asking?
The head is not more native to the heart,
The hand more instrumental to the mouth,

---

[74] *Disjoint* for *disjointed.* The Poet has many preterites so formed.

[75] *Colleaguèd* does not refer to, or, as we should say, agree with *Fortinbras*, but with *supposal*, or rather with the whole sense of the three preceding lines. So that the meaning is, "his supposal of our weakness, or of our unsettled condition, *united* with his expectation of advantage."

[76] *Band* and *bond* were the same, and both used for *obligation.*

[77] *Gait* is *course, progress*; which is much the same as *walk.—In that* has the sense of *because* or *inasmuch as.* Often so.

[78] *To* was often thus used where we should use *for.* So a little before, in "taken *to* wife," and a little after in "bow them *to* your gracious leave."

[79] The scope of these articles when dilated or explained in full. Such elliptical expressions are common with the Poet. Modern grammar would require *allows* instead of *allow.*

[80] That is, cannot speak *what is reasonable.*

Than is the throne of Denmark to thy father.[81]
What wouldst thou have, Laertes?
LAERTES. My dread lord,
   Your leave and favour to return to France;
   From whence though willingly I came to Denmark,
   To show my duty in your coronation,
   Yet now, I must confess, that duty done,
   My thoughts and wishes bend again toward France
   And bow them to your gracious leave and pardon.
KING. Have you your father's leave? What says Polonius?
POLONIUS. He hath, my lord, wrung from me my slow leave
   By laboursome petition, and at last
   Upon his will I seal'd my hard[82] consent:
   I do beseech you, give him leave to go.
KING. Take thy fair hour, Laertes; time be thine,
   And thy best graces spend it at thy will![83]
   But now, my cousin Hamlet, and my son—
HAMLET. [*Aside.*] A little more than kin, and less than kind.[84]
KING. How is it that the clouds still hang on you?
HAMLET. Not so, my lord; I am too much in the sun.[85]
QUEEN. Good Hamlet, cast thy nighted colour off,
   And let thine eye look like a friend on Denmark.
   Do not for ever with thy vailed lids[86]
   Seek for thy noble father in the dust:
   Thou know'st 'tis common—all that lives must die,

---

[81] The various parts of the body enumerated are not more *allied, more necessary* to each other, than the King of Denmark is bound to your father to do him service.

[82] *Hard* for *reluctant, difficult*; like *slow* just before.

[83] "Take an auspicious hour, Laertes; be your time your own, and thy best virtues guide thee in spending of it at thy will."

[84] The King is "a little more than kin" to Hamlet, because, in being at once his uncle and his father, he is *twice* kin. And he is "less than kind," because his incestuous marriage, as Hamlet views it, is *unnatural* or *out of nature*. The Poet repeatedly uses *kind* in its primitive sense of *nature*. Professor Himes, however, of Gettysburg, Penn., questions this explanation, and writes me as follows: "It seems to me that, since Hamlet has just been addressed as cousin and as son, he is still the object of thought, and the words quoted must be referred by the Prince to himself, and not to the King. In other words, it is Hamlet who is 'a little more than kin, and less than kind.' If we take *kin* as a substitute for *cousin*, and *kind* as a substitute for *son*, Hamlet is a little more than the first, for he is nephew, and a little less than the second, for he is only a step-son. Hamlet's *aside* is thus a retort upon the King's words; as though he said, 'I am neither the one nor the other,—a little more than the one, and not so much as the other.'"

[85] Hamlet seems to have a twofold meaning here. First, he intends a sort of antithesis to the King's, "How is it that the clouds still hang on you?" Second, he probably alludes to the old proverbial phrase of being *in the sun*, or *in the warm sun*, which used to signify the state of being without the charities of home and kindred,— exposed to the social inclemencies of the world. Hamlet regards himself as exiled from these charities, as having lost both father and mother.

[86] With *downcast eyes.* To *vail* is to *lower*, to *let fall*.

Passing through nature to eternity.
HAMLET. Ay, madam, it is common.
QUEEN. If it be,
    Why seems it so particular with thee?
HAMLET. Seems, madam! Nay it is; I know not 'seems.'
    'Tis not alone my inky cloak, good mother,
    Nor customary suits of solemn black,
    Nor windy suspiration of forced breath,
    No, nor the fruitful river in the eye,
    Nor the dejected haviour of the visage,
    Together with all forms, moods, shapes of grief,
    That can denote me truly: these indeed seem,
    For they are actions that a man might play;
    But I have that within which passes show—
    These but the trappings and the suits of woe.
KING. 'Tis sweet and commendable in your nature, Hamlet,
    To give these mourning duties to your father:
    But, you must know, your father lost a father;
    That father lost, lost his, and the survivor bound
    In filial obligation for some term
    To do obsequious[87] sorrow: but to persever
    In obstinate condolement is a course
    Of impious stubbornness; 'tis unmanly grief;
    It shows a will most incorrect[88] to heaven,
    A heart unfortified, a mind impatient,
    An understanding simple and unschool'd;
    For what we know must be and is as common
    As any the most vulgar thing to sense,
    Why should we in our peevish opposition
    Take it to heart? Fie! 'tis a fault to heaven,
    A fault against the dead, a fault to nature,
    To reason most absurd: whose common theme
    Is death of fathers, and who still hath cried,
    From the first corpse till he that died to-day,
    'This must be so.' We pray you, throw to earth
    This unprevailing[89] woe, and think of us
    As of a father: for let the world take note,
    You are the most immediate to our throne;
    And with no less nobility of love
    Than that which dearest father bears his son,
    Do I impart toward you.[90] For your intent

[87] The Poet uses *obsequious* as having the sense of *obsequies.*
[88] *Incorrect* is here used in the sense or *incorrigible.*
[89] *Unprevailing* was used in the sense of *unavailing.*
[90] "Impart towards you," seems rather odd language, especially as *impart* has no

In going back to school in Wittenberg,[91]
It is most retrograde to our desire:
And we beseech you, bend you to remain
Here, in the cheer and comfort of our eye,
Our chiefest courtier, cousin, and our son.
QUEEN. Let not thy mother lose her prayers, Hamlet:
I pray thee, stay with us; go not to Wittenberg.
HAMLET. I shall in all my best obey you, madam.
KING. Why, 'tis a loving and a fair reply:
Be as ourself in Denmark. Madam, come;
This gentle and unforced accord of Hamlet
Sits smiling to my heart: in grace whereof,
No jocund health that Denmark drinks to-day,
But the great cannon to the clouds shall tell,
And the king's rouse the heavens all bruit again,[92]
Re-speaking earthly thunder. Come away.

[*Flourish. Exeunt all but* HAMLET.]

HAMLET. O, that this too too solid flesh would melt
Thaw and resolve[93] itself into a dew!
Or that the Everlasting had not fix'd
His canon 'gainst self-slaughter! O God! God!
How weary, stale, flat and unprofitable,
Seem to me all the uses of this world!
Fie on't! ah fie! 'tis an unweeded garden,
That grows to seed; things rank and gross in nature
Possess it merely.[94] That it should come to this!
But two months dead: nay, not so much, not two:
So excellent a king; that was, to this,
Hyperion to a satyr;[95] so loving to my mother

---

object. The meaning probably is, "I take you into a partnership," or, "I invest you with a participation of the royal dignity, as heir-presumptive."—"Nobility of love" is merely a generous or heightened phrase for *love.*

[91] *School* was applied to places not only of academical, but also of professional study; and in the olden time men were wont to spend their whole lives in such cloistered retirements of learning. So that we need not suppose Hamlet was "going back to school" as an undergraduate.

[92] A *rouse* was a deep draught to one's health, wherein it was the custom to empty the cup or goblet. Its meaning was the same as *carouse.* To *bruit* is to *noise;* used with *again,* the same as *echo* or *reverberate.*

[93] *Resolve* in its old sense of *dissolve.* The three words *melt, thaw,* and *resolve,* all signifying the same thing, are used merely for emphasis.

[94] *Merely* in one of the Latin senses of *mere; wholly, entirely.*

[95] *Hyperion,* which literally means *sublimity,* was one of the names of Apollo, the most beautiful of all the gods, and much celebrated in classic poetry for his golden locks. Here, as often, *to* has the force of *compared to.*

That he might not beteem[96] the winds of heaven
Visit her face too roughly. Heaven and earth!
Must I remember? why, she would hang on him,
As if increase of appetite had grown
By what it fed on: and yet, within a month—
Let me not think on't. Frailty, thy name is woman!—
A little month, or e'er[97] those shoes were old
With which she followed my poor father's body,
Like Niobe, all tears[98]—why she, even she—
O, God! a beast, that wants discourse of reason,[99]
Would have mourn'd longer—married with my uncle,
My father's brother, but no more like my father
Than I to Hercules: within a month:
Ere yet the salt of most unrighteous tears
Had left the flushing[100] in her galled eyes,
She married. O, most wicked speed, to post
With such dexterity to incestuous sheets!
It is not nor it cannot come to good:
But break, my heart; for I must hold my tongue.

[*Enter* HORATIO, MARCELLUS, *and* BERNARDO.]

HORATIO. Hail to your lordship!
HAMLET. I am glad to see you well:
    Horatio,—or I do forget myself.
HORATIO. The same, my lord, and your poor servant ever.
HAMLET. Sir, my good friend; I'll change that name with you:[101]
    And what make you[102] from Wittenberg, Horatio? Marcellus?
MARCELLUS. My good lord—
HAMLET. I am very glad to see you.—[*To* BERNARDO.] Good even,
    sir.[103]

---

[96] *Beteem* is an old word for *permit* or *suffer*.

[97] *Or ever* was in common use for *before, sooner than.*

[98] Niobe was the wife of Amphion, King of Thebes. As she had twelve children, she went to crowing one day over Latona, who had only two, Apollo and Diana. In return for this, all her twelve were slain by Latona's two; and Jupiter, in pity of her sorrow, transformed her into a rock, from which her tears issued in a perennial stream.

[99] *Discourse of reason*, in old philosophical language, is *rational* discourse, or *discursive* reason; the faculty of pursuing a train of thought, or of passing from thought to thought in the way of inference or conclusion.

[100] Shakespeare has *leave* repeatedly in the sense of *leave off*, or *cease. Flushing* is the redness of the eyes caused by what the Poet elsewhere calls "eye-offending brine."

[101] As if he had said, "No, not my poor servant: we are *friends*; that is the style I will exchange with you."

[102] "What *make* you?" is old language for "What *do* you?"

[103] The words, *Good even, sir*, are evidently addressed to Bernardo, whom Hamlet has not before known; but, as he now meets him in company with old acquaintances, like

But what, in faith, make you from Wittenberg?
HORATIO. A truant disposition, good my lord.
HAMLET. I would not hear your enemy say so,
    Nor shall you do mine ear that violence,
    To make it truster of your own report
    Against yourself: I know you are no truant.
    But what is your affair in Elsinore?
    We'll teach you to drink deep ere you depart.
HORATIO. My lord, I came to see your father's funeral.
HAMLET. I pray thee, do not mock me, fellow-student;
    I think it was to see my mother's wedding.
HORATIO. Indeed, my lord, it followed hard upon.
HAMLET. Thrift, thrift,[104] Horatio! the funeral baked meats
    Did coldly furnish forth the marriage tables.
    Would I had met my dearest[105] foe in heaven
    Or ever I had seen that day, Horatio!
    My father—methinks I see my father.
HORATIO. Where, my lord?
HAMLET. In my mind's eye, Horatio.
HORATIO. I saw him once; he was a goodly king.
HAMLET. He was a man, take him for all in all,
    I shall not look upon his like again.
HORATIO. My lord, I think I saw him yesternight.
HAMLET. Saw? who?
HORATIO. My lord, the king your father.
HAMLET. The king my father!
HORATIO. Season your admiration[106] for awhile
    With an attent ear, till I may deliver,
    Upon the witness of these gentlemen,
    This marvel to you.
HAMLET. For God's love, let me hear.
HORATIO. Two nights together had these gentlemen,
    Marcellus and Bernardo, on their watch,
    In the dead vast[107] and middle of the night,
    Been thus encount'red. A figure like your father,
    Armed at point exactly, cap-a-pe,

---

a true gentleman, he gives him a salutation of kindness.—Marcellus has said before of Hamlet, "I this *morning* know where we shall find him." But *good even* was the common salutation after noon.

[104] *Thrift* means *economy*: all was done merely to save cost.

[105] In Shakespeare's time *dearest* was applied to any person or thing that excites the liveliest interest, whether of love or hate.

[106] *Admiration* in the Latin sense of *wonder* or *astonishment.—Season* is *qualify* or *temper.*

[107] *Vast* is *void* or *vacancy*. So in *The Tempest*, i. 2: "Urchins shall, for that *vast* of night that they may work," &c.

Appears before them, and with solemn march
Goes slow and stately by them: thrice he walk'd
By their oppress'd and fear-surprised eyes,
Within his truncheon's length; whilst they, distilled
Almost to jelly with the act of fear,[108]
Stand dumb and speak not to him. This to me
In dreadful secrecy impart they did;
And I with them the third night kept the watch;
Where, as they had delivered, both in time,
Form of the thing, each word made true and good,
The apparition comes: I knew your father;
These hands are not more like.
HAMLET. But where was this?
MARCELLUS. My lord, upon the platform where we watch'd.
HAMLET. Did you not speak to it?
HORATIO. My lord, I did;
But answer made it none: yet once methought
It lifted up its head and did address
Itself to motion, like as it would speak;
But even then the morning cock crew loud,
And at the sound it shrunk in haste away,
And vanish'd from our sight.
HAMLET. 'Tis very strange.
HORATIO. As I do live, my honour'd lord, 'tis true;
And we did think it writ down in our duty
To let you know of it.
HAMLET. Indeed, indeed, sirs, but this troubles me.
Hold you the watch to-night?
ALL. We do, my lord.
HAMLET. Arm'd, say you?
ALL. Arm'd, my lord.
HAMLET. From top to toe?
ALL. My lord, from head to foot.
HAMLET. Then saw you not his face?
HORATIO. O, yes, my lord; he wore his beaver up.[109]
HAMLET. What, look'd he frowningly?
HORATIO. A countenance more in sorrow than in anger.
HAMLET. Pale or red?
HORATIO. Nay, very pale.
HAMLET. And fix'd his eyes upon you?

---

[108] To *distill* is to fall in drops, to melt; so that *distill'd* is a very natural and fit expression for the cold sweat caused by intense fear. "The *act* of fear" is the *action* or the *effect* of fear.

[109] The beaver was a movable part of the helmet, which could be drawn down over the face or pushed up over the forehead.

HORATIO. Most constantly.
HAMLET. I would I had been there.
HORATIO. It would have much amazed you.
HAMLET. Very like, very like. Stay'd it long?
HORATIO. While one with moderate haste might tell[110] a hundred.
BOTH. Longer, longer.
HORATIO. Not when I saw't.
HAMLET. His beard was grizzled—no?
HORATIO. It was, as I have seen it in his life,
    A sable silver'd.
HAMLET. I will watch to-night;
    Perchance 'twill walk again.
HORATIO. I warrant it will.
HAMLET. If it assume my noble father's person,
    I'll speak to it, though hell itself should gape
    And bid me hold my peace. I pray you all,
    If you have hitherto conceal'd this sight,
    Let it be tenable[111] in your silence still;
    And whatsoever else shall hap to-night,
    Give it an understanding, but no tongue:
    I will requite your loves. So, fare you well:
    Upon the platform, 'twixt eleven and twelve,
    I'll visit you.
ALL. Our duty to your honour.
HAMLET. Your loves, as mine to you: farewell.

[*Exeunt all but* HAMLET.]

My father's spirit in arms! All is not well;
I doubt[112] some foul play: would the night were come!
Till then sit still, my soul. Foul deeds will rise,
Though all the earth o'erwhelm them, to men's eyes. [*Exit.*]

---

[110] To *tell* was continually used for *count.*

[111] *Tenable* for *retained.* The Poet has many like instances of confusion of forms; as *admired* for *admirable*, that is, *wonderful*, in *Macbeth*, iii. 4: "Broke the good meeting with most *admired* disorder."

[112] *Doubt* in the sense of *fear* or *suspect.* Repeatedly so.

SCENE III.

The Same. A Room in POLONIUS's *house.*

[*Enter* LAERTES *and* OPHELIA.][113]

LAERTES. My necessaries are embark'd. Farewell.
And, sister, as the winds give benefit
And convoy[114] is assistant, do not sleep,
But let me hear from you.[115]
OPHELIA. Do you doubt that?
LAERTES. For Hamlet and the trifling of his favour,
Hold it a fashion and a toy in blood,
A violet in the youth of primy nature,
Forward, not permanent, sweet, not lasting,
The perfume and suppliance of a minute;[116]
No more.
OPHELIA. No more but so?
LAERTES. Think it no more;[117]
For nature, crescent, does not grow alone
In thews[118] and bulk, but, as this temple waxes,
The inward service of the mind and soul
Grows wide withal.[119] Perhaps he loves you now,
And now no soil nor cautel[120] doth besmirch
The virtue of his will: but you must fear,
His greatness weigh'd, his will is not his own;
For he himself is subject to his birth:[121]
He may not, as unvalued persons do,

---

[113] This scene must be regarded as one of Shakespeare's lyric movements in the play, and the skill with which it is interwoven with the dramatic parts is peculiarly an excellence with our Poet. *You experience the sensation of a pause, without the sense of a stop.*—COLERIDGE.

[114] *Convoy* for *conveyance.* Communication with France being by sea, there needed both a ship to carry letters, and a wind to drive the ship.

[115] That is, "*without letting* me hear from you." The Poet repeatedly uses *but* in this way.

[116] A mere pastime, to *supply* or *fill up* the passing hour; a sweet play, to beguile the present idle time. Instead of *supplyance,* the Poet elsewhere has *supplyment* in much the same sense.

[117] "Take for granted that such is the case, till you have clear proof to the contrary."—*Crescent is growing, increasing.*

[118] *Thews* for *sinews* or *muscles.*

[119] The idea is, that Hamlet's love is but a youthful fancy, which, as his mind comes to maturity, he will outgrow. The passage would seem to infer that the Prince is not so old as he is elsewhere represented to be.

[120] *Cautel* is a debauched relation of *caution,* and means *fraud* or *deceit.*

[121] Subject to the *conditions* which his birth entails upon him.

Carve for himself; for on his choice depends
The safety and health of this whole state;
And therefore must his choice be circumscribed
Unto the voice and yielding of that body
Whereof he is the head.[122] Then if he says he loves you,
It fits your wisdom so far to believe it
As he in his particular act and place
May give his saying deed;[123] which is no further
Than the main voice of Denmark goes withal.
Then weigh what loss your honour may sustain,
If with too credent ear you list his songs,[124]
Or lose your heart, or your chaste treasure open
To his unmast'red importunity.
Fear it, Ophelia, fear it, my dear sister,
And keep you in the rear of your affection,
Out of the shot and danger of desire.
The chariest maid is prodigal enough,
If she unmask her beauty to the moon:
Virtue itself scapes not calumnious strokes:
The canker galls the infants of the spring,
Too oft before their buttons be disclosed,[125]
And in the morn and liquid dew of youth
Contagious blastments are most imminent.
Be wary then; best safety lies in fear:
Youth to itself rebels, though none else near.

OPHELIA. I shall the effect of this good lesson keep,
As watchman to my heart. But, good my brother,
Do not, as some ungracious pastors[126] do,
Show me the steep and thorny way to heaven;
Whiles, like a puff'd and reckless libertine,
Himself the primrose path of dalliance treads,
And recks not his own read.[127]

LAERTES. O, fear me not.
I stay too long: but here my father comes.

[*Enter* POLONIUS.]

---

[122] His choice must be limited by the approval or consent of the nation.

[123] So far only as he, in his public and official character, shall make his promise good.

[124] "If with too *credulous* ear you *listen to* his songs."

[125] In Shakespeare's time, *canker* was often used of the worm that kills the early buds before they open out into flowers. Perhaps it here means a rust that sometimes infests plants, and *eats* out their life.—*Buttons* is *buds,* and *disclose* is used in the sense of *open* or *unfold.*

[126] Pastors that *have not the grace* to practice what they preach.

[127] *Regards* not his own *lesson.*

A double blessing is a double grace,
Occasion smiles upon a second leave.
POLONIUS. Yet here, Laertes! aboard, aboard, for shame!
The wind sits in the shoulder of your sail,
And you are stay'd for. There; my blessing with thee!
And these few precepts in thy memory
See thou character.[128] Give thy thoughts no tongue,
Nor any unproportion'd thought his act.[129]
Be thou familiar, but by no means vulgar.[130]
Those friends thou hast, and their adoption tried,
Grapple them to thy soul with hoops of steel;
But do not dull thy palm with entertainment
Of each new-hatch'd, unfledged comrade.[131] Beware
Of entrance to a quarrel, but being in,
Bear't that the opposed may beware of thee.
Give every man thy ear, but few thy voice;
Take each man's censure,[132] but reserve thy judgment.
Costly thy habit as thy purse can buy,
But not express'd in fancy; rich, not gaudy;
For the apparel oft proclaims the man,
And they in France of the best rank and station
Are of a most select and generous chief in that.[133]
Neither a borrower nor a lender be;
For loan oft loses both itself and friend,
And borrowing dulls the edge of husbandry.
This above all—to thine own self be true,
And it must follow, as the night the day,
Thou canst not then be false to any man.[134]

---

[128] To *character* is to *engrave* or *imprint*.

[129] *Unproportion'd* for *unhandsome* or *unfitting. His*, again, for *its*.

[130] *Vulgar* is here used in its old sense of *common*.

[131] "Do not *blunt* thy feeling by taking every new acquaintance by the hand, or by admitting him to the intimacy of a friend."

[132] *Censure* was continually used for *opinion*, or *judgment*.

[133] That is, most select and generous, but chiefly or especially so in the matter of dress.

[134] This is regarded by many as a very high strain of morality. I cannot see it so; though, to be sure, it is as high as Polonius can go: it is the height of worldly wisdom,—a rule of being wisely selfish. In the same sense, "honesty is the best policy"; but no truly honest man ever acts on that principle. A *passion* for rectitude is the only thing that will serve. It is indeed true that we have duties, indispensable duties, to ourselves; that a man ought to be wise for himself. But that the being wise for one's self is the first and highest duty, I do not believe. And the man who makes that the first principle of morality never will and never can be truly wise for himself. Such, however, is the first principle of Polonius's morality; and it is in perfect keeping with the whole of his thoroughly selfish and sinister mind. But he just loses himself by acting upon it. Aiming first of all to be true to himself, he has been utterly false to himself and to his family. Faith, or allegiance, to

Farewell; my blessing season[135] this in thee!
LAERTES. Most humbly do I take my leave, my lord.
POLONIUS. The time invites you; go; your servants tend.
LAERTES. Farewell, Ophelia; and remember well
    What I have said to you.
OPHELIA. 'Tis in my memory lock'd,
    And you yourself shall keep the key of it.
LAERTES. Farewell. [*Exit.*]
POLONIUS. What is't, Ophelia, be hath said to you?
OPHELIA. So please you, something touching the Lord Hamlet.
POLONIUS. Marry, well bethought:
    'Tis told me, he hath very oft of late
    Given private time to you; and you yourself
    Have of your audience been most free and bounteous:
    If it be so,—as so 'tis put on me,
    And that in way of caution—I must tell you,
    You do not understand yourself so clearly
    As it behooves my daughter and your honour.
    What is between you? Give me up the truth.
OPHELIA. He hath, my lord, of late made many tenders
    Of his affection to me.
POLONIUS. Affection! pooh! you speak like a green girl,
    Unsifted[136] in such perilous circumstance.
    Do you believe his tenders, as you call them?
OPHELIA. I do not know, my lord, what I should think.
POLONIUS. Marry, I'll teach you: think yourself a baby;
    That you have ta'en these tenders for true pay,
    Which are not sterling. Tender yourself more dearly;[137]
    Or—not to crack the wind of the poor phrase,
    Running it thus[138]—you'll tender me a fool.
OPHELIA. My lord, he hath importuned me with love

---

stand secure, must needs fasten upon something out of and above self. If Polonius had said, "Be true to God, to your country, or to your kind, and it must follow, as the night the day, thou canst not then be false unto thyself," he would have uttered a just and noble thing; but then it would have been quite out of character, and in discord with the whole tenour of his speech. And the old wire-puller, with his double-refined ethics of selfishness, has nothing venerable about him; while the baseness of Laertes seems to me the legitimate outcome of such moral teachings as these contained so pithily in his father's benediction.

[135] *Season* is here used, apparently, in the sense of *ingrain*; the idea being that of so *steeping* the counsel into his mind that it will not fade out.

[136] *Unsifted* is *untried, inexperienced.* We still speak of *sifting* a matter.

[137] Polonius is using *tender* in different senses; first in a business or financial sense, as in the phrase "legal tender"; then in the sense of being careful of a thing, or of holding it precious or dear.

[138] Polonius is likening the phrase to a poor nag, which, if run too hard, will be *wind-broken.*

In honourable fashion.
POLONIUS. Ay, fashion you may call it; go to, go to.
OPHELIA. And hath given countenance to his speech, my lord,
With almost all the holy vows of heaven.
POLONIUS. Ay, springes to catch woodcocks.[139] I do know,
When the blood burns, how prodigal the soul
Lends the tongue vows: these blazes, daughter,
Giving more light than heat, extinct in both,
Even in their promise, as it is a-making,
You must not take for fire. From this time
Be somewhat scanter of your maiden presence;
Set your entreatments at a higher rate
Than a command to parley.[140] For Lord Hamlet,
Believe so much in him, that he is young
And with a larger tether[141] may he walk
Than may be given you: in few,[142] Ophelia,
Do not believe his vows; for they are brokers,[143]
Not of that dye which their investments show,
But mere implorators of unholy suits,
Breathing like sanctified and pious bawds,[144]
The better to beguile. This is for all—
I would not, in plain terms, from this time forth,
Have you so slander[145] any moment leisure,
As to give words or talk with the Lord Hamlet.
Look to't, I charge you: come your ways.
OPHELIA. I shall obey, my lord. [*Exeunt.*]

---

[139] This was a proverbial phrase. There is a collection of epigrams under that title; the woodcock being accounted a witless bird, from a vulgar notion that it had no brains. "Springes to catch woodcocks" means arts to entrap simplicity. *Springe* is, properly, *snare* or *trap.—Blood*, in the next line, is put *for passion.* Often so.

[140] Be more difficult of access, and let the *suits to you* for that purpose be of higher respect than a command to talk or chat.

[141] A *longer line*; a horse, fastened by a string to a stake, is *tethered.*

[142] In few *words*; in *short.*

[143] *Brokers*, as the word is here used, are *go-betweens*, or *panders*; the same as *bawds*, a little after.

[144] This joining of words that are really contradictory, or qualifying of a noun with adjectives that literally quench it, sometimes gives great strength of expression.

[145] That is, so disgrace, or misuse, as to *cause* slander.

SCENE IV.

The Same. A Platform before the Castle.

[*Enter* HAMLET, HORATIO, *and* MARCELLUS.]

HAMLET. The air bites shrewdly; it is very cold.
HORATIO. It is a nipping and an eager[146] air.
HAMLET. What hour now?
HORATIO. I think it lacks of twelve.
HAMLET. No, it is struck.
HORATIO. Indeed? I heard it not: then it draws near the season
    Wherein the spirit held his wont to walk.

[*A flourish of trumpets, and two pieces go off.*]

    What does this mean, my lord?
HAMLET. The king doth wake to-night and takes his rouse,[147]
    Keeps wassail, and the swaggering up-spring reels;[148]
    And, as he drains his draughts of Rhenish down,
    The kettle-drum and trumpet thus bray out
    The triumph of his pledge.
HORATIO. Is it a custom?
HAMLET. Ay, marry, is't;
    But to my mind, though I am native here
    And to the manner born, it is a custom
    More honour'd in the breach than the observance.
    This heavy-headed revel east and west[149]
    Makes us traduced and tax'd of other nations;
    They clepe us drunkards, and with swinish phrase
    Soil our addition;[150] and indeed it takes

---

[146] *Eager* was used in the sense of the French *aigre*, sharp, biting.

[147] To *wake* is to *hold a late revel* or *debauch*. A *rouse* is what we now call a *bumper.*—*Wassail* originally meant a drinking to one's health; hence it came to be used for any festivity of the bottle and the bowl.

[148] Reels *through* the swaggering *up-spring*, which was the name of a rude, boisterous German dance, as appears from a passage in Chapman's *Alphonsus*: "We Germans have no changes in our dances; an almain and an *upspring*, that is all."

[149] The sense of *east and west* goes with what follows, not what precedes: "brings reproach upon us in all directions." To *tax* was often used so.

[150] *Clepe* is an old Saxon word for *call.*—The Poet often uses *addition* for *title*; so that the meaning is, they sully our title by likening us to swine. The character here ascribed to the Danes appears to have had a basis of fact. Heywood, in his *Drunkard Opened*, 1635, speaking of "the vinosity of nations," says the Danes have made profession thereof from antiquity, and are the first upon record "that have brought their wassel bowls and elbow-deep healths into this land."

From our achievements, though perform'd at height,
The pith and marrow of our attribute.[151]
So, oft it chances in particular men,[152]
That for some vicious mole of nature in them,
As, in their birth, wherein they are not guilty,
Since nature cannot choose his origin;
By the o'ergrowth of some complexion,
Oft breaking down the pales and forts of reason,[153]
Or by some habit that too much o'er-leavens
The form of plausive[154] manners—that these men,
Carrying, I say, the stamp of one defect,
Being nature's livery, or fortune's star,[155]
Their virtues else, be they as pure as grace,
As infinite as man may undergo,
Shall in the general censure take corruption
From that particular fault. The dram of eale
Doth all the noble substance of a doubt
To his own scandal.[156]

[*Enter the* GHOST.]

HORATIO. Look, my lord, it comes!
HAMLET. Angels and ministers of grace defend us!

---

[151] That is, of our *reputation*, or of what *is attributed* to us.

[152] Hamlet is now wrought up to the highest pitch of expectancy; his mind is sitting on thorns; and he seeks relief from the pain of that overintense feeling by launching off into a strain of general and abstract reflection. His state of mind, distracted between his eager anticipation and his train of thought, aptly registers itself in the irregular and broken structure of his language.

[153] The idea is, of some native aptitude indulged and fostered too much, so that it breaks down the proper guards and strongholds of reason. Here, as in some other cases, *pales* is *palings*. And *complexion* was often used, as here, to signify any constitutional *texture, aptitude,* or *predisposition.*

[154] *Plausive* for *approvable*, or that which is to be applauded; the active form with the passive sense. This indiscriminate use of active and passive forms was very common.

[155] Alluding to the old astrological notion, of a man's character or fortune being determined by the star that was in the ascendant on the day of his birth.—*Livery* is properly a *badge-dress*; here put for a man's *distinctive idiom.*—Note the change of the subject from *these men* to *their virtues.*

[156] *His*, again, for *its*, referring to *substance*, or, possibly, to *leav'n*. Of course *'em* refers to *virtues*. So that the meaning is, that the dram of leaven sours all the noble substance of their virtues, insomuch as to bring reproach and scandal on that substance itself. The Poet seems to have had in mind Saint Paul's saying, *i Corinthians*, v. 6: "A little leaven leaveneth the whole lump." And so in Bacon's *Henry the Seventh*: "And, as a little *leaven* of new distaste doth commonly *soure* the whole lumpe of former *merites*, the King's wit began now to suggest unto his passion," &c. This is said in reference to Sir William Stanley, whose prompt and timely action gained the victory of Bosworth Field. Some years after, he became a suitor for the earldom of Chester; whereupon, as Bacon says, "his suit did end not only in a denial, but in a *distaste*" on the part of the King.

Be thou a spirit of health or goblin damn'd,
Bring with thee airs from heaven or blasts from hell,
Be thy intents wicked or charitable,
Thou com'st in such a questionable[157] shape
That I will speak to thee: I'll call thee Hamlet,
King, father, royal Dane: O, answer me!
Let me not burst in ignorance; but tell
Why thy canonized bones, hearsed in death,
Have burst their cerements;[158] why the sepulchre,
Wherein we saw thee quietly enurn'd,
Hath op'd his ponderous and marble jaws,
To cast thee up again. What may this mean,
That thou, dead corpse, again in complete steel
Revisits thus the glimpses of the moon,
Making night hideous; and we fools of nature
So horridly to shake our disposition
With thoughts beyond the reaches of our souls?[159]
Say, why is this? wherefore? what should we do?

[GHOST *beckons* HAMLET.]

HORATIO. It beckons you to go away with it,
    As if it some impartment did desire
    To you alone.
MARCELLUS. Look, with what courteous action
    It waves you to a more removed ground:
    But do not go with it.
HORATIO. No, by no means.
HAMLET. It will not speak; then I will follow it.
HORATIO. Do not, my lord.
HAMLET. Why, what should be the fear?
    I do not set my life in a pin's fee;
    And for my soul, what can it do to that,
    Being a thing immortal as itself?
    It waves me forth again: I'll follow it.
HORATIO. What if it tempt you toward the flood, my lord,
    Or to the dreadful summit of the cliff

---

[157] "A *questionable* shape" is a shape that may be *questioned*, or *conversed with*. In like manner the Poet often uses *question* for *conversation*.

[158] *Canonized* means made sacred by the *canonical* rites of sepulture.—*Cerements* is a dissyllable. It is from a Latin word meaning *wax*, and was so applied from the use of wax or pitch in sealing up coffins or caskets.

[159] "We fools of Nature," in the sense here implied, is, we who cannot by nature know the mysteries of the supernatural world. Strict grammar would require *us* instead of *we*.—The general idea of the passage seems to be, that man's intellectual eye is not strong enough to bear the unmuffled light of eternity.

That beetles o'er his base[160] into the sea,
And there assume some other horrible form,
Which might deprive your sovereignty of reason[161]
And draw you into madness?[162] think of it:
The very place puts toys[163] of desperation,
Without more motive, into every brain
That looks so many fathoms to the sea
And hears it roar beneath.
HAMLET. It waves me still.
Go on; I'll follow thee.
MARCELLUS. You shall not go, my lord.
HAMLET. Hold off your hands.
HORATIO. Be ruled; you shall not go.
HAMLET. My fate cries out,
And makes each petty artery[164] in this body
As hardy as the Nemean lion's nerve. [GHOST *beckons.*]
Still am I call'd. Unhand me, gentlemen.

[*Breaking from them.*]

By heaven, I'll make a ghost of him that lets[165] me!
I say, away! Go on; I'll follow thee.

[*Exeunt* GHOST *and* HAMLET.]

HORATIO. He waxes desperate with imagination.
MARCELLUS. Let's follow; 'tis not fit thus to obey him.
HORATIO. Have after. To what issue will this come?
MARCELLUS. Something is rotten in the state of Denmark.
HORATIO. Heaven will direct it.
MARCELLUS. Nay,[166] let's follow him. [*Exeunt.*]

---

[160] *Overhangs its* base. So in Sidney's *Arcadia*: "Hills lift up their *beetle* brows, as if they would overlooke the pleasantnesse of their under prospect."

[161] To "deprive your sovereignity of reason" is to *depose* your *government* of reason, or take it away. The word was often used thus.

[162] It was anciently believed that evil spirits sometimes assumed the guise of deceased persons, to draw men into madness and suicide, as is here apprehended of the Ghost.

[163] *Toys* is *freaks*, *whims*, or *fancies*, here meaning any sudden mad impulse to suicide.

[164] *Artery*, *nerve*, and *sinew* were used interchangeably in the Poet's time.

[165] The old *let*, now obsolete, meaning to *hinder*.

[166] *Nay* refers to Horatio's "Heaven will direct it," and means, "let us not leave it to Heaven, but look after it ourselves."

SCENE V.

Another Part of the Platform.

[*Enter the* GHOST *and* HAMLET.]

HAMLET. Where wilt thou lead me? Speak; I'll go no further.
GHOST. Mark me.
HAMLET. I will.
GHOST. My hour is almost come,
    When I to sulphurous and tormenting flames
    Must render up myself.
HAMLET. Alas, poor ghost!
GHOST. Pity me not, but lend thy serious hearing
    To what I shall unfold.
HAMLET. Speak; I am bound to hear.
GHOST. So art thou to revenge, when thou shalt hear.
HAMLET. What?
GHOST. I am thy father's spirit,
    Doom'd for a certain term to walk the night,
    And for the day confined to fast in fires,[167]
    Till the foul crimes done in my days of nature
    Are burnt and purged away. But that I am forbid
    To tell the secrets of my prison-house,
    I could a tale unfold whose lightest word
    Would harrow up thy soul, freeze thy young blood,
    Make thy two eyes, like stars, start from their spheres,
    Thy knotted and combined locks to part
    And each particular hair to stand on end,
    Like quills upon the fretful porpentine.[168]
    But this eternal[169] blazon must not be
    To ears of flesh and blood. List, list, O, list!
    If thou didst ever thy dear father love—
HAMLET. O God!
GHOST. Revenge his foul and most unnatural murder.
HAMLET. Murder!
GHOST. Murder most foul, as in the best it is;

---

[167] Chaucer in the *Persones Tale* says, "The misese of hell shall be *in defaute of mete and drinke.*" So, too, in *The Wyll of the Devyll*: "Thou shalt lye in frost and fire, with sicknes and *hunger.*"

[168] Such is the old form of the word, and so Shakespeare always has it.

[169] The Poet repeatedly has *eternal* in the sense of *infernal*, like our Yankee '*tarnal*; and such is probably the meaning here; though some think it means "the mysteries of eternity."

But this most foul, strange and unnatural.

HAMLET. Haste me to know't, that I, with wings as swift
As meditation or the thoughts of love,
May sweep to my revenge.

GHOST. I find thee apt;
And duller shouldst thou be than the fat weed
That roots itself in ease on Lethe wharf,[170]
Wouldst thou not stir in this. Now, Hamlet, hear:
'Tis given out that, sleeping in my orchard,[171]
A serpent stung me; so the whole ear of Denmark
Is by a forged process of my death
Rankly abused: but know, thou noble youth,
The serpent that did sting thy father's life
Now wears his crown.

HAMLET. O my prophetic soul![172]
My uncle!

GHOST. Ay, that incestuous, that adulterate beast,
With witchcraft of his wit, with traitorous gifts—
O wicked wit and gifts, that have the power
So to seduce!—won to his shameful lust
The will of my most seeming-virtuous queen:
O Hamlet, what a falling-off was there!
From me, whose love was of that dignity
That it went hand in hand even with the vow
I made to her in marriage, and to decline
Upon a wretch whose natural gifts were poor
To[173] those of mine!
But virtue, as it never will be moved,
Though lewdness court it in a shape of heaven,
So lust, though to a radiant angel link'd,
Will sate itself in a celestial bed,
And prey on garbage.
But, soft! methinks I scent the morning air;
Brief let me be. Sleeping within my orchard,
My custom always of the afternoon,
Upon my secure[174] hour thy uncle stole,
With juice of cursed hebenon[175] in a vial,

---

[170] Of course "Lethe wharf" is the place on the banks of the river Lethe where the old boatman, Charon, had his moorings.—In the preceding line, *shouldst* for *wouldst*.

[171] *Orchard* and *garden* were synonymous.

[172] Hamlet has suspected "some foul play," and now his suspicion seems prophetic, or as if inspired.

[173] *To*, again, for *compared to*.

[174] *Secure* has the sense of the Latin *securus*; *unguarded, unsuspecting*.

[175] *Hebenon* is probably derived from *henbane*, the oil of which, according to Pliny, dropped into the ears, disturbs the brain; and there is sufficient evidence that it was held

And in the porches of my ears did pour
The leperous distilment; whose effect[176]
Holds such an enmity with blood of man
That swift as quicksilver it courses through
The natural gates and alleys of the body,[177]
And with a sudden vigour doth posset
And curd, like eager[178] droppings into milk,
The thin and wholesome blood: so did it mine;
And a most instant tetter bark'd[179] about,
Most lazar-like, with vile and loathsome crust,
All my smooth body.
Thus was I, sleeping, by a brother's hand
Of life, of crown, of queen, at once dispatch'd;
Cut off even in the blossoms of my sin,
Unhousel'd, disappointed, unanel'd;[180]
No reckoning made, but sent to my account
With all my imperfections on my head:
HAMLET. O, horrible! O, horrible! most horrible!
GHOST. If thou hast nature[181] in thee, bear it not;
Let not the royal bed of Denmark be
A couch for luxury and damned incest.
But, howsoever thou pursuest this act,
Taint not thy mind,[182] nor let thy soul contrive
Against thy mother aught; leave her to heaven
And to those thorns that in her bosom lodge,
To prick and sting her. Fare thee well at once!
The glow-worm shows the matin to be near,
And 'gins to pale his uneffectual[183] fire:

---

poisonous. So in Anton's *Satires*, 1606: "The *poison'd henbane*, whose cold juice doth kill."

[176] *Effect* for *efficacy*, or *effectiveness*; the effect put for the cause.

[177] The Poet here implies as much as was then known touching the circulation of the blood. The lawyers claim Shakespeare as of their house; I suspect the physicians have an equal right to him.

[178] *Eager* has occurred before in the sense of *sharp, biting.* "Eager droppings" are drops of *acid.*

[179] *Bark'd* means *formed a bark* or *scab.—Instant* in the sense of the Latin *instans; urgent, importunate, itching.—*The meaning of *lazar-like* is well illustrated in *Paradise Lost,* xi. 477-488.

[180] *Unhousell'd* is without having received the sacrament. *Disappointed* is *unappointed, unprepared.* A man well-furnished for an enterprise is said to be well-*appointed. Unanel'd* is without extreme unction. So in Cavendish's *Life of Wolsey:* "Then we began to put him in mind of Christ's passion; and sent for the abbot of the place to *anneal* him. These "last offices" were thought to mitigate the pains of Purgatory.

[181] *Nature* for *natural affection.* A very frequent usage.

[182] This part of the injunction is well worth noting: time and manner are left to Hamlet; only he is to keep himself clean from crime and from dishonour: his revenge must be righteous, and according to the demands of justice, not merely personal.

Adieu, adieu! Hamlet, remember me.

[*Exit* GHOST.]

HAMLET. O all you host of heaven! O earth! what else?
And shall I couple hell? O, fie![184] Hold, hold, my heart;
And you, my sinews, grow not instant old,
But bear me stiffly up. Remember thee!
Ay, thou poor ghost, while memory holds a seat
In this distracted globe.[185] Remember thee!
Yea, from the table[186] of my memory
I'll wipe away all trivial fond records,
All saws of books, all forms, all pressures past,
That youth and observation copied there;
And thy commandment all alone shall live
Within the book and volume of my brain,
Unmix'd with baser matter: yes, by heaven!
O most pernicious woman!
O villain, villain, smiling, damned villain!
My tables,[187]—meet it is I set it down,
That one may smile, and smile, and be a villain;
At least I'm sure it may be so in Denmark.—
So, uncle, there you are.[188] Now to my word;
It is 'Adieu, adieu! remember me.'
I have sworn't.
HORATIO. [*Within.*] My lord, my lord,—
MARCELLUS. [*Within.*] Lord Hamlet!
HORATIO. [*Within.*] Heaven secure him!
HAMLET. [*Within.*] So be it!
HORATIO. [*Within.*] Hillo, ho, ho, my lord!
HAMLET. Hillo, ho, ho, boy! come, bird, come.[189]

---

[183] *Uneffectual* because it gives light without heat, does not *burn.*—*Matin,* properly morning-prayers, is here put for *morning.*

[184] Hamlet invokes Heaven and Earth, and then asks if he shall invoke Hell also. "O, fie!" refers to the latter, and implies a strong negative.

[185] By *this globe* Hamlet means his *head.*

[186] *Table* for *tablet.*—*Saws* is *sayings; pressures, impressions.*

[187] "*Tables,* or books, or registers for memory of things" were used in Shakespeare's time by all ranks of persons, and carried in the pocket; what we call *memorandum-books.*

[188] This, I think, has commonly been taken in too literal and formal a way, as if Hamlet were carefully writing down the axiomatic saying he has just uttered. I prefer Professor Werder's view of the matter: "Hamlet pulls out his tablets, and jabs the point of his pencil once or twice into the leaf, because he cannot do the same to the King with his sword, as he would like to do,—nothing further; only such marks, such a sign, does he make. That stands for 'So, uncle, there you are!' And although he says he must write it down for himself, he does not literally write; that does not accord with his mood and situation."

[*Enter* HORATIO *and* MARCELLUS.]

MARCELLUS. How is't, my noble lord?
HORATIO. What news, my lord?
HAMLET. O, wonderful!
HORATIO. Good my lord, tell it.
HAMLET. No; you'll reveal it.
HORATIO. Not I, my lord, by heaven.
MARCELLUS. Nor I, my lord.
HAMLET. How say you, then; would heart of man once think it?
    But you'll be secret?
BOTH. Ay, by heaven, my lord.
HAMLET. There's ne'er a villain dwelling in all Denmark
    But he's an arrant knave.[190]
HORATIO. There needs no ghost, my lord, come from the grave
    To tell us this.
HAMLET. Why, right; you are i' the right;
    And so, without more circumstance[191] at all,
    I hold it fit that we shake hands and part:
    You, as your business and desire shall point you;
    For every man has business and desire,
    Such as it is; and for mine own poor part,
    Look you, I'll go pray.
HORATIO. These are but wild and whirling words, my lord.
HAMLET. I'm sorry they offend you, heartily;
    Yes, faith heartily.
HORATIO. There's no offence, my lord.
HAMLET. Yes, by Saint Patrick,[192] but there is, Horatio,
    And much offence too. Touching this vision here—
    It is an honest ghost,[193] that let me tell you.
    For your desire to know what is between us,
    O'ermaster't[194] as you may. And now, good friends,

---

[189] This is the call which falconers use to their hawk in the air when they would have him come down to them.

[190] Dr. Isaac Ray, a man of large science and ripe experience in the treatment of insanity, says of Hamlet's behaviour in this scene, that "it betrays the excitement of delirium,—the wandering of a mind reeling under the first stroke of disease."

[191] *Circumstance* is sometimes used for *circumlocution*. But it was also used for *circumstantial detail*; and such is probably the meaning here.

[192] Warburton has ingeniously defended Shakespeare for making the Danish Prince swear by *St. Patrick*, by observing that the whole northern world had their learning from Ireland.

[193] Hamlet means that the Ghost is a real ghost, just what it appears to be, and not "the Devil" in "a pleasing shape," as Horatio had apprehended it to be.

[194] That is, o'ermaster your *desire*; "subdue it as you best can."

As you are friends, scholars and soldiers,
Give me one poor request.
HORATIO. What is't, my lord? We will.
HAMLET. Never make known what you have seen to-night.
BOTH. My lord, we will not.
HAMLET. Nay, but swear't.
HORATIO. In faith,
My lord, not I.
MARCELLUS. Nor I, my lord, in faith.
HAMLET. Upon my sword.
MARCELLUS. We have sworn, my lord, already.[195]
HAMLET. Indeed, upon my sword, indeed.
GHOST. [*Beneath.*] Swear.
HAMLET. Ah, ha, boy! say'st thou so? art thou there, truepenny?[196]
Come on. You hear this fellow in the cellarage.
Consent to swear.
HORATIO. Propose the oath, my lord.
HAMLET. Never to speak of this that you have seen,
Swear by my sword.
GHOST. [*Beneath.*] Swear.
HAMLET. Hic et ubique? then we'll shift our ground.
Come hither, gentlemen,
And lay your hands again upon my sword:
Never to speak of this that you have heard,
Swear by my sword.
GHOST. [*Beneath.*] Swear.
HAMLET. Well said, old mole! canst work i' the earth so fast?
A worthy pioneer![197] Once more remove, good friends.
HORATIO. O day and night, but this is wondrous strange!
HAMLET. And therefore as a stranger give it welcome.
There are more things in heaven and earth, Horatio,
Than are dreamt of in your philosophy.[198]
But come;

---

[195] The oath they have already sworn is *in faith*. But this has not enough of ritual solemnity in it, to satisfy Hamlet. The custom of swearing by the Sword, or rather by the cross at the hilt of it, is very ancient. The Saviour's name was sometimes inscribed on the handle. So that swearing by one's sword was the most solemn oath a Christian soldier could take.

[196] *True-penny* is an old familiar term for a right honest fellow.

[197] Alluding to one of the offices of military engineers, which is to *pioneer* an army; that is, to go before and clear the road.

[198] Strictly speaking, *your* is redundant here. Hamlet means *any* philosophy. The Poet often uses the pronouns in that way. So in v. 1, of this play: "And *your* water is a sore decayer of *your* whoreson dead body." In the text, however, I suspect that *your* is meant to convey a mild sneer at philosophy, which has sometimes been as arrogant as science is in some of her modern representatives.

Here, as before, never, so help you mercy,
How strange or odd some'er I bear myself,
As I perchance hereafter shall think meet
To put an antic disposition on,[199]
That you, at such times seeing me, never shall,
With arms encumb'red thus, or this headshake,
Or by pronouncing of some doubtful phrase,
As 'Well, well, we know,' or 'We could, an if we would,'
Or 'If we list to speak,' or 'There be, an if they might,'
Or such ambiguous giving out, to note
That you know aught of me: this not to do,
So grace and mercy at your most need help you, Swear.
GHOST. [*Beneath.*] Swear.
HAMLET. Rest, rest, perturbed spirit!—[*They swear.*] So, gentlemen,
With all my love I do commend me to you;
And what so poor a man as Hamlet is
May do, to express his love and friending to you,
God willing, shall not lack. Let us go in together;
And still your fingers on your lips, I pray.
The time is out of joint: O cursed spite,
That ever I was born to set it right!
Nay, come, let's go together. [*Exeunt.*]

---

[199] This has been taken as proving that Hamlet's "antic disposition" is merely assumed for a special purpose. But our ripest experts in the matter are far from regarding it so. They tell us that veritable madmen are sometimes inscrutably cunning in arts for disguising their state; saying, in effect, "To be sure, you may find me acting rather strangely at times, but I know what I am about, and have a purpose in it."

ACT II.

SCENE I.

Elsinore. The house of POLONIUS.

[*Enter* POLONIUS *and* REYNALDO.]

POLONIUS. Give him this money and these notes, Reynaldo.
REYNALDO. I will, my lord.
POLONIUS. You shall do marvellous wisely, good Reynaldo,
    Before you visit him, to make inquire
    Of his behavior.
REYNALDO. My lord, I did intend it.
POLONIUS. Marry, well said; very well said. Look you, sir,
    Inquire me first what Danskers[200] are in Paris;
    And how, and who, what means, and where they keep,[201]
    What company, at what expense; and finding
    By this encompassment and drift of question
    That they do know my son, come you more nearer
    Than your particular demands will touch it:[202]
    Take you, as 'twere, some distant knowledge of him;
    As thus, 'I know his father and his friends,
    And in part him'. Do you mark this, Reynaldo?
REYNALDO. Ay, very well, my lord.
POLONIUS. 'And in part him; but' you may say 'not well:'
    But, if't be he I mean, he's very wild;
    Addicted so and so. And there put on him
    What forgeries you please; marry, none so rank
    As may dishonour him; take heed of that;
    But, sir, such wanton, wild and usual slips
    As are companions noted and most known
    To youth and liberty.
REYNALDO. As gaming, my lord.
POLONIUS. Ay, or drinking, fencing, swearing, quarrelling,
    Drabbing: you may go so far.

---

[200] *Dansker* is *Dane*; *Dansk* being the ancient name of Denmark.—Here *me* is used very much *as your* in the preceding scene.

[201] The Poet repeatedly uses *keep* in the sense of *lodge* or *dwell*.

[202] This seems illogical, and would be so in any mouth but a politician's, as implying that general inquiries would come to the point faster than particular ones. But here, again, *your* is used as explained in note 198. The scheme here laid down is, to *steal* upon the truth by roundabout statements and questions; or, as it is afterwards said, "By indirections find directions out."

REYNALDO. My lord, that would dishonour him.
POLONIUS. Faith, no; as you may season it in the charge
    You must not put another scandal on him,
    That he is open to incontinency;[203]
    That's not my meaning: but breathe his faults so quaintly[204]
    That they may seem the taints of liberty,
    The flash and outbreak of a fiery mind,
    A savageness in unreclaimed blood,
    Of general assault.[205]
REYNALDO. But, my good lord,—
POLONIUS. Wherefore should you do this?
REYNALDO. Ay, my lord,
    I would know that.
POLONIUS. Marry, sir, here's my drift;
    And I believe, it is a fetch of warrant:[206]
    You laying these slight sullies on my son,
    As 'twere a thing a little soil'd i' the working, Mark you,
    Your party in converse, him you would sound,
    Having ever seen in the prenominate crimes
    The youth you breathe of guilty,[207] be assured
    He closes with you in this consequence;
    'Good sir,' or so, or 'friend,' or 'gentleman,'
    According to the phrase or the addition
    Of man and country.
REYNALDO. Very good, my lord.
POLONIUS. And then, sir, does he this—'a does—what was I about to say? By the Mass,[208] I was about to say something: where did I leave?
REYNALDO. At 'closes in the consequence,' at 'friend or so,' and 'gentleman.'
POLONIUS. At 'closes in the consequence,' ay, marry;

---

[203] The emphasis, here, is on *open*, and *of is* equivalent to *in respect of.* So that the meaning is, "You must not put *the further* scandal upon him, that he is *openly* incontinent, or that he indulges his passions publicly and 'with unbashful forehead,' as this would argue him to be shameless." Polonius justly thinks that good appearances are worth something, and that, in a shameless vice, the shamelessness is the worst part of it; there being then nothing for amendment to fasten upon.—Perhaps I should add, that here, again, *season* is *qualify* or *mitigate.*

[204] *Quaintly,* from the Latin *comptus,* properly means *elegantly,* but is here used in the sense of *adroitly* or *ingeniously.*

[205] A wildness of untamed blood, such as youth is generally assailed by.

[206] "A fetch of warrant" is an allowable stratagem or artifice.

[207] Having *at any time* seen the youth you *speak* of guilty in the *forenamed vices.*— "Closes with you in this consequence" means, apparently, *agrees* with you in this *conclusion.—Addition* again for *title.*

[208] *Mass* is the old name of the Lord's Supper, and is still used by the Roman Catholics. It was often sworn by, as in this instance.

He closes thus: 'I know the gentleman;
I saw him yesterday, or t' other day,
Or then, or then; with such, or such; and, as you say,
There was a' gaming; there o'ertook in's rouse;
There falling out at tennis:' or perchance,
'I saw him enter such a house of sale,'
Videlicet, a brothel, or so forth.
See you now;
Your bait of falsehood takes this carp of truth:[209]
And thus do we of wisdom and of reach,
With windlasses and with assays of bias,[210]
By indirections find directions out:
So by my former lecture and advice,
Shall you my son. You have me, have you not?[211]
REYNALDO. My lord, I have.
POLONIUS. God be wi' you;[212] fare you well.
REYNALDO. Good my lord!
POLONIUS. Observe his inclination in yourself.[213]
REYNALDO. I shall, my lord.
POLONIUS. And let him ply his music.[214]
REYNALDO. Well, my lord.
POLONIUS. Farewell! [*Exit* REYNALDO.]

[*Enter* OPHELIA.]

How now, Ophelia! what's the matter?
OPHELIA. O, my lord, my lord, I have been so affrighted!
POLONIUS. With what, i' the name of God?

---

[209] Polonius is fond of angling arts. The *carp* is a species of fish.

[210] "Of wisdom and of reach" is here equivalent to *by cunning and overreaching.—Windlaces* is here used in the sense of taking a winding, circuitous, or roundabout course to a thing, instead of going *directly* to it; or, as we sometimes say, "beating about the bush," instead of coming straight to the point. This is shown by a late writer in *The Edinburgh Review*, who quotes from Golding's translation of Ovid:

> The winged god, beholding them returning in a troupe,
> Continu'd not directly forth, but gan me down to stoupe
> And fetch'd a *windlass* round about.

"Assays of bias" are *trials* of *inclination.* A bias is a weight in one side of a bowl, which keeps it from rolling straight to the mark, as in ninepins.

[211] "You *understand* me, do you not?"

[212] The old phrase, "God be with you," is here in the process of abbreviation to what we now use, "Good-bye."

[213] "Use your own eyes upon him, as well as learn from others." Or the meaning may be, "comply with his inclinations in order to draw him out." *Observe* sometimes has this sense of *yielding to*, and *so flattering.*

[214] "Eye him sharply, but *slyly*, and let him fiddle his secrets all out."

OPHELIA. My lord, as I was sewing in my closet,
    Lord Hamlet, with his doublet all unbrac'd;[215]
    No hat upon his head; his stockings fouled,
    Ungart'red, and down-gyved to his ankle;[216]
    Pale as his shirt; his knees knocking each other;
    And with a look so piteous in purport
    As if he had been loosed out of hell
    To speak of horrors—he comes before me.
POLONIUS. Mad for thy love?
OPHELIA. My lord, I do not know;
    But truly, I do fear it.
POLONIUS. What said he?
OPHELIA. He took me by the wrist and held me hard;
    Then goes he to the length of all his arm;
    And, with his other hand thus o'er his brow,
    He falls to such perusal of my face
    As he would draw it.[217] Long stay'd he so;
    At last, a little shaking of mine arm
    And thrice his head thus waving up and down,
    He raised a sigh so piteous and profound
    As it did seem to shatter all his bulk[218]
    And end his being: that done, he lets me go,
    And, with his head over his shoulder turn'd,
    He seem'd to find his way without his eyes;
    For out o' doors he went without their helps,
    And, to the last, bended their light on me.
POLONIUS. Come, go with me: I will go seek the king.
    This is the very ecstasy of love,
    Whose violent property fordoes[219] itself
    And leads the will to desperate undertakings
    As oft as any passion under heaven
    That does afflict our natures. I am sorry.
    What, have you given him any hard words of late?
OPHELIA. No, my good lord, but, as you did command,
    I did repel his fetters and denied
    His access to me.
POLONIUS. That hath made him mad.
    I am sorry that with better heed and judgment

---

[215] *Unbraced* is the same as our *unbuttoned.*

[216] Hanging down like the loose cincture that confines the fetters or gyves round the ankles.

[217] "To such a *study* of my face as *if* he would *make a picture* of it."

[218] Here *bulk* is put for *breast.* The usage was common.

[219] All through this play, *ecstasy* is *madness.* It was used for any violent perturbation of mind.—*Fordo* was the same as *undo* or *destroy.*

I had not quoted[220] him. I fear'd he did but trifle,
And meant to wreck thee; but, beshrew[221] my jealousy!
By heaven, it is as proper to our age
To cast beyond ourselves in our opinions[222]
As it is common for the younger sort
To lack discretion.[223] Come, go we to the king:
This must be known; which, being kept close, might move
More grief to hide than hate to utter love.[224] [*Exeunt.*]

SCENE II.

The Same. A Room in the Castle.

[*Flourish. Enter the* KING, *the* QUEEN, ROSENCRANTZ,
GUILDENSTERN, *and Attendants.*]

KING. Welcome, dear Rosencrantz and Guildenstern!
Moreover that[225] we much did long to see you,
The need we have to use you did provoke
Our hasty sending. Something have you heard
Of Hamlet's transformation; so call it,
Sith nor the exterior nor the inward man
Resembles that it was. What it should be,
More than his father's death, that thus hath put him
So much from the understanding of himself,
I cannot dream of. I entreat you both,
That, being of so young days brought up with him,
And sith so neighboured to his youth and humour,[226]
That you vouchsafe your rest here in our court
Some little time: so by your companies
To draw him on to pleasures, and to gather,
So much as from occasion you may glean,

---

[220] To *quote* is to *note*, to *mark*, or *observe*.

[221] *Beshrew* was much used as a mild form of imprecation; about the same as *confound* it! or, *a plague upon* it!

[222] In this admirable scene, Polonius, who is throughout the skeleton of his former skill in state-craft, hunts the trail of policy at a dead scent, supplied by the weak fever-smell in his own nostrils.—COLERIDGE.

[223] We old men are as apt to overreach ourselves with our own policy, as the young are to miscarry through inconsideration.

[224] The sense is rather obscure, but appears to be, "By keeping Hamlet's love secret, we may cause more of grief to others, than of hatred on his part by disclosing it." The Poet sometimes strains language pretty hard in order to close a scene with a rhyme. The infinitives are here gerundial.

[225] *Moreover that* for *besides that.* Not so elsewhere, I think.

[226] And having since had so near an opportunity of studying his inclination and character during his youth.

    Whether aught, to us unknown, afflicts him thus,
    That, open'd, lies within our remedy.
QUEEN. Good gentlemen, he hath much talk'd of you;
    And sure I am two men there are not living
    To whom he more adheres. If it will please you
    To show us so much gentry[227] and good will
    As to expend your time with us awhile,
    For the supply and profit of our hope,[228]
    Your visitation shall receive such thanks
    As fits a king's remembrance.
ROSENCRANTZ. Both your majesties
    Might, by the sovereign power you have of us,
    Put your dread pleasures more into command
    Than to entreaty.
GUILDENSTERN. But we both obey,
    And here give up ourselves, in the full bent
    To lay our service freely at your feet,
    To be commanded.
KING. Thanks, Rosencrantz and gentle Guildenstern.
QUEEN. Thanks, Guildenstern and gentle Rosencrantz:
    And I beseech you instantly to visit
    My too much changed son. Go, some of you,
    And bring these gentlemen where Hamlet is.
GUILDENSTERN. Heavens make our presence and our practices
    Pleasant and helpful to him!
QUEEN. Ay, amen!

      [*Exeunt* ROSENCRANTZ, GUILDENSTERN, *and some*
        Attendants.]

      [*Enter* POLONIUS.]

POLONIUS. The ambassadors from Norway, my good lord,
    Are joyfully return'd.
KING. Thou still hast been the father of good news.
POLONIUS. Have I, my lord? I assure my good liege,
    I hold my duty, as I hold my soul,
    Both to my God and to my gracious King:[229]
    And I do think, or else this brain of mine
    Hunts not the trail of policy so sure
    As it hath used to do, that I have found

---

[227] *Gentry* for *courtesy, gentleness,* ox *good-breeding.*
[228] "The supply and profit" is *the feeding* and *realizing.*
[229] "I hold my duty both to my God and to my King, as I do my soul."

The very cause of Hamlet's lunacy.
KING. O, speak of that; that do I long to hear.
POLONIUS. Give first admittance to the ambassadors;
    My news shall be the fruit to that great feast.
KING. Thyself do grace to them, and bring them in.

[*Exit* POLONIUS.]

He tells me, my dear Gertrude, he hath found
The head and source of all your son's distemper.
QUEEN. I doubt it is no other but the main;[230]
    His father's death, and our o'erhasty marriage.
KING. Well, we shall sift him.

[*Re-enter* POLONIUS, *with* VOLTEMAND *and* CORNELIUS.]

Welcome, my good friends!
Say, Voltemand, what from our brother Norway?
VOLTEMAND. Most fair return of greetings and desires.
    Upon our first, he sent out to suppress
    His nephew's levies; which to him appear'd
    To be a preparation 'gainst the Polack;
    But, better look'd into, he truly found
    It was against your highness: whereat grieved,
    That so his sickness, age and impotence
    Was falsely borne in hand,[231] sends out arrests
    On Fortinbras; which he, in brief, obeys;
    Receives rebuke from Norway, and in fine
    Makes vow before his uncle never more
    To give the assay of arms against your majesty.
    Whereon old Norway, overcome with joy,
    Gives him three thousand crowns in annual fee,[232]
    And his commission to employ those soldiers,
    So levied as before, against the Polack:
    With an entreaty, herein further shown, [*Gives a paper.*]
    That it might please you to give quiet pass
    Through your dominions for this enterprise,
    On such regards of safety and allowance[233]

---

[230] *Doubt*, again, for *suspect* or *fear.*—*Main* seems to be here used for *matter of chief interest*, the thing or things with which people's thoughts have been mainly occupied.

[231] To *bear in hand* is to delude or impose upon by false assurances.

[232] *Fee* was often used for *fee-simple*, which is the strongest tenure in English law, and means an estate held in absolute right.

[233] That is, on such *pledges* of safety to the country, and on such *terms* of

As therein are set down.
KING. It likes us well;[234]
  And at our more consider'd time[235] well read,
  Answer, and think upon this business.
  Meantime we thank you for your well-took labour:
  Go to your rest; at night we'll feast together:
  Most welcome home! [*Exeunt* VOLTEMAND *and* CORNELIUS.]
POLONIUS. This business is well ended.
  My liege, and madam, to expostulate[236]
  What majesty should be, what duty is,
  Why day is day, night night, and time is time,
  Were nothing but to waste night, day and time.
  Therefore, since brevity is the soul of wit,
  And tediousness the limbs and outward flourishes,
  I will be brief: your noble son is mad:
  Mad call I it; for, to define true madness,
  What is't but to be nothing else but mad?
  But let that go.
QUEEN. More matter, with less art.
POLONIUS. Madam, I swear I use no art at all.
  That he is mad, 'tis true: 'tis true 'tis pity;
  And pity, 'tis true: a foolish figure;
  But farewell it, for I will use no art.
  Mad let us grant him, then: and now remains
  That we find out the cause of this effect,
  Or rather say, the cause of this defect,
  For this effect defective comes by cause:
  Thus it remains, and the remainder thus.
  Perpend.[237]
  I have a daughter—have while she is mine—
  Who, in her duty and obedience, mark,
  Hath given me this: now gather, and surmise.
  [*Reads.*] 'To the celestial and my soul's idol, the most beautified
  Ophelia.' That's an ill phrase, a vile phrase; 'beautified' is a vile
  phrase: but you shall hear. Thus:
  [*Reads.*] 'In her excellent white bosom, these,[238] & c.'

---

permission. The passage of an army through a country is apt to cause great trouble and damage to the people.

[234] "It likes us" for "it pleases us," or "we like it." Often so.

[235] That is, "when we have had time for *further consideration!*" The Poet has several like expressions in this play.

[236] *Expostulate* in the Latin sense of *argue* or *discuss*.

[237] *Perpend* is *weigh* or *consider*.

[238] The word *these* was usually added at the end of the superscription of letters. Hamlet's letter is somewhat in the euphuistic style which was fashionable in the Poet's time.

QUEEN. Came this from Hamlet to her?
POLONIUS. Good madam, stay awhile; I will be faithful.

[*Reads.*]   'Doubt thou the stars are fire;
            Doubt that the sun doth move;
            Doubt truth to be a liar;
            But never doubt I love.

'O dear Ophelia, I am ill at these numbers; I have not art to reckon[239] my groans: but that I love thee best, O most best, believe it. Adieu.

            'Thine evermore most dear lady, whilst this
                  machine is to him,[240] HAMLET.'

This, in obedience, hath my daughter shown me,
And more above, hath his solicitings,
As they fell out by time, by means and place,
All given to mine ear.
KING. But how hath she
Received his love?
POLONIUS. What do you think of me?
KING. As of a man faithful and honourable.
POLONIUS. I would fain prove so. But what might you think,
When I had seen this hot love on the wing,
As I perceived it, I must tell you that,
Before my daughter told me—what might you,
Or my dear majesty your queen here, think,
If I had play'd the desk or table-book,[241]
Or given my heart a winking, mute and dumb,[242]
Or look'd upon this love with idle sight;
What might you think? No, I went round[243] to work,
And my young mistress thus I did bespeak:
'Lord Hamlet is a prince, out of thy star;[244]
This must not be:' and then I precepts gave her,

---

[239] Hamlet is *tacitly* quibbling: he first uses *numbers* in the sense of *verses*, and here *implies* the other sense.

[240] That is, "while he is living." *Machine* for *body*; as the body is framed, and works, upon strictly-mechanical principles.

[241] By keeping dark about the matter. A desk or table-book does not prate of what it contains. A table-book is a case or set of tablets, to carry in the pocket, and write memoranda upon.

[242] "If I had given my heart a *hint* to be mute about their passion." "Conniventia, *a winking at*, a sufferance; *a feigning not to see or* know."

[243] To be *round* is to be *plain, downright, outspoken*.

[244] Not within thy *destiny*; alluding to the supposed influence of the stars on the fortune of life.

That she should lock herself from his resort,
Admit no messengers, receive no tokens.
Which done, she took the fruits of my advice;
And he, repelled, a short tale to make,
Fell into a sadness, then into a fast,
Thence to a watch, thence into a weakness,
Thence to a lightness, and, by this declension,
Into the madness wherein now he raves,
And all we mourn for.
KING. Do you think 'tis this?
QUEEN. It may be, very likely.
POLONIUS. Hath there been such a time—I would fain know that—
That I have positively said 'Tis so,'
When it proved otherwise?
KING. Not that I know.
POLONIUS. [*Pointing to his head and shoulder.*] Take this from this,
if this be otherwise:
If circumstances lead me, I will find
Where truth is hid, though it were hid indeed
Within the centre.[245]
KING. How may we try it further?
POLONIUS. You know, sometimes he walks four hours together
Here in the lobby.
QUEEN. So he does indeed.
POLONIUS. At such a time I'll loose my daughter to him:
Be you and I behind an arras[246] then;
Mark the encounter: if he love her not
And be not from his reason fall'n thereon,
Let me be no assistant for a state,
But keep a farm and carters.
KING. We will try it.
QUEEN. But, look, where sadly the poor wretch[247] comes reading.
POLONIUS. Away, I do beseech you, both away:
I'll board[248] him presently.—

[*Exeunt* KING, QUEEN and ATTENDANTS.]

---

[245] *Centre* here means, no doubt, the Earth, which, in the old astronomy, was held to be literally the centre of the solar system.

[246] In Shakespeare's time the chief rooms of houses were lined with tapestry hangings, which were suspended some distance from the walls, to keep them from being rotted by the damp.

[247] *Wretch* was the strongest term of endearment in the language; generally implying, however, a dash of pity.

[248] To *board* him is to *accost* or *address* him.

[*Enter* HAMLET, *reading.*]

O, give me leave.

How does my good Lord Hamlet?

HAMLET. Well, God-a-mercy.

POLONIUS. Do you know me, my lord?

HAMLET. Excellent well; you are a fishmonger.[249]

POLONIUS. Not I, my lord.

HAMLET. Then I would you were so honest a man.

POLONIUS. Honest, my lord!

HAMLET. Ay, sir; to be honest, as this world goes, is to be one man picked out of ten thousand.

POLONIUS. That's very true, my lord.

HAMLET. For if the sun breed maggots in a dead dog, being a god kissing carrion[250]—

Have you a daughter?

POLONIUS. I have, my lord.

HAMLET. Let her not walk i' the sun: conception is a blessing: but not as your daughter may conceive. Friend, look to 't.

POLONIUS. How say you by that?[251]—[*Aside.*] Still harping on my daughter: yet he knew me not at first; he said I was a fishmonger: he is far gone, far gone: and truly in my youth I suffered much extremity for love; very near this. I'll speak to him again.—What do you read, my lord?

HAMLET. Words, words, words.

POLONIUS. What is the matter, my lord?

HAMLET. Between who?

POLONIUS. I mean, the matter that you read, my lord.

HAMLET. Slanders, sir: for the satirical rogue says here that old men have grey beards, that their faces are wrinkled, their eyes purging thick amber and plum-tree gum and that they have a plentiful lack of wit, together with most weak hams: all which, sir, though I most powerfully and potently believe, yet I hold it not honesty[252] to have

---

[249] *Fishmonger* meant an angler as well as a dealer in fish. Hamlet probably means that Polonius has come to *fish out* his secret.—*God-a-mercy*, second line before, is an old colloquialism, commonly meaning "God *have* mercy": here it means "*thank* God"; *mercy* being used just as in the French *grand merci*.

[250] "A good *kissing* carrion" is, no doubt, a carrion good *for kissing*, or good to *kiss*. So in *The Merry Wives*, v. 5, we have "*kissing-comfits*," which were candies flavoured so as to perfume the breath, and render the lips sweet for kissing. And so we often say "good hay-making weather," meaning, of course, weather good for hay-making, or good to make hay.

[251] "*How say* you by that?" is "*What do* you *mean* by that?"

[252] Shakespeare sometimes uses *honesty* with the sense of the adjective *right*, or *honourable*.

it thus set down, for yourself, sir, should be old as I am, if like a
   crab you could go backward.[253]
POLONIUS. [*Aside.*] Though this be madness, yet there is method
   in't.—Will you walk out of the air, my lord?
HAMLET. Into my grave.
POLONIUS. Indeed, that is out o' the air.—[*Aside.*] How pregnant[254]
   sometimes his replies are! a happiness that often madness hits on,
   which reason and sanity could not so prosperously be delivered of.
   I will leave him, and suddenly contrive the means of meeting
   between him and my daughter.—My lord, I will most humbly take
   my leave of you.
HAMLET. You cannot, sir, take from me any thing that I will more
   willingly part withal—except my life, except my life,—[*Aside.*]
   except my life.

[*Enter* ROSENCRANTZ *and* GUILDENSTERN.]

POLONIUS. Fare you well, my lord.
HAMLET. These tedious old fools!
POLONIUS. You go to seek the Lord Hamlet; there he is.
ROSENCRANTZ. [*To* POLONIUS.] God save you, sir!

[*Exit* POLONIUS.]

GUILDENSTERN. My honour'd lord!
ROSENCRANTZ. My most dear lord!
HAMLET. My excellent good friends! How dost thou,
   Guildenstern? Ah, Rosencrantz! Good lads, how do ye both?
ROSENCRANTZ. As the indifferent[255] children of the earth.
GUILDENSTERN. Happy, in that we are not over-happy;
   On fortune's cap we are not the very button.
HAMLET. Nor the soles of her shoe?
ROSENCRANTZ. Neither, my lord.
HAMLET. Then you live about her waist, or in the middle of her
   favours?
GUILDENSTERN. Faith, her privates we.
HAMLET. In the secret parts of fortune? O, most true; she is a
   strumpet. What's the news?
ROSENCRANTZ. None, my lord, but that the world's grown honest.
HAMLET. Then is doomsday near: but your news is not true. Let me
   question more in particular: what have you, my good friends,

---

[253] That is, "if you could *turn your life* backward, and grow young."

[254] *Pregnant*, here, is pithy, *full of meaning*, or of *pertinency.*

[255] *Indifferent*, here, has the sense of *middling,—tolerably well-off.*

deserved at the hands of fortune, that she sends you to prison hither?

GUILDENSTERN. Prison, my lord!

HAMLET. Denmark's a prison.

ROSENCRANTZ. Then is the world one.

HAMLET. A goodly one; in which there are many confines, wards and dungeons, Denmark being one o' the worst.

ROSENCRANTZ. We think not so, my lord.

HAMLET. Why, then, 'tis none to you; for there is nothing either good or bad, but thinking makes it so: to me it is a prison.

ROSENCRANTZ. Why then, your ambition makes it one; 'tis too narrow for your mind.

HAMLET. O God, I could be bounded in a nut shell and count myself a king of infinite space, were it not that I have bad dreams.

GUILDENSTERN. Which dreams indeed are ambition, for the very substance of the ambitious[256] is merely the shadow of a dream.

HAMLET. A dream itself is but a shadow.

ROSENCRANTZ. Truly, and I hold ambition of so airy and light a quality that it is but a shadow's shadow.

HAMLET. Then are our beggars bodies, and our monarchs and outstretched heroes the beggars' shadows. Shall we to the court? for, by my fay, I cannot reason.[257]

BOTH. We'll wait upon you.

HAMLET. No such matter: I will not sort you with the rest of my servants, for, to speak to you like an honest man, I am most dreadfully attended.[258] But, in the beaten way of friendship, what make you at Elsinore?[259]

ROSENCRANTZ. To visit you, my lord; no other occasion.

---

[256] This is obscure: but "the very substance of the ambitious" probably means the substance of *that which* the ambitious *pursue*, not that of which they *are made*. The obscurity grows from an uncommon use of the objective genitive. The passage reminds me of Burke's well-known saying, "What shadows we are, and what shadows we pursue!"

[257] Hamlet is here playing or fencing with words, and seems to lose himself in the riddles he is making. The meaning is any thing but clear; perhaps was not meant to be understood. But *bodies* is probably put for *substance* or *substances*; and the sense appears to turn partly upon the fact that *substance* and *shadow* are antithetic and correlative terms, as there can be no shadow without a substance to cast it. So the best comment I have met with is Dr. Bucknill's: "If ambition is but a shadow, something beyond ambition must be the substance from which it is thrown. If ambition, represented by a king, is a shadow, the antitype of ambition, represented by a beggar, must be the opposite of the shadow, that is, the substance."—The word *outstretched* infers, apparently, that the Poet had in mind the sculptured images of heroic kings lying in death, such as were in old times much used for monuments.—*Fay* is merely a diminutive of *faith*.

[258] Referring, perhaps, to the "bad dreams" spoken of a little before.

[259] "What *is your business* at Elsinore?"

HAMLET. Beggar that I am, I am even poor in thanks; but I thank you:
and sure, dear friends, my thanks are too dear a halfpenny. Were
you not sent for? Is it your own inclining? Is it a free visitation?
Come, deal justly with me: come, come; nay, speak.

GUILDENSTERN. What should we say, my lord?

HAMLET. Why, any thing, but to the purpose. You were sent for; and
there is a kind of confession in your looks which your modesties
have not craft enough to colour:²⁶⁰ I know the good king and queen
have sent for you.

ROSENCRANTZ. To what end, my lord?

HAMLET. That you must teach me. But let me conjure you, by the
rights of our fellowship, by the consonancy of our youth, by the
obligation of our ever-preserved love, and by what more dear a
better proposer could charge you withal, be even and direct with
me, whether you were sent for, or no?.

ROSENCRANTZ. [*Aside to* GUILDENSTERN.] What say you?

HAMLET. [*Aside.*] Nay, then, I have an eye of you.²⁶¹—If you love
me, hold not off.

GUILDENSTERN. My lord, we were sent for.

HAMLET. I will tell you why; so shall my anticipation prevent your
discovery, and your secrecy to the king and queen moult no
feather.²⁶² I have of late—but wherefore I know not—lost all my
mirth, forgone all custom of exercises; and indeed it goes so
heavily with my disposition that this goodly frame, the earth,
seems to me a sterile promontory, this most excellent canopy, the
air, look you, this brave²⁶³ o'er-hanging firmament, this majestical
roof fretted with golden fire, why, it appears no other thing to me
than a foul and pestilent congregation of vapours. What a piece of
work is a man! how noble in reason! how infinite in faculty! in
form and moving how express and admirable! in action how like
an angel! in apprehension how like a god! the beauty of the world!
the paragon of animals! And yet, to me, what is this quintessence
of dust? man delights not me: no, nor woman neither, though by
your smiling you seem to say so.

ROSENCRANTZ. My lord, there was no such stuff in my thoughts.

HAMLET. Why did you laugh then, when I said 'man delights not
me'?

---

²⁶⁰ To *colour* is to *disguise*, or *conceal.*

²⁶¹ "I will watch you sharply." *Of* for *on*; a common usage.

²⁶² Hamlet's fine sense of honour is well shown in this. He will not tempt them to
any breach of confidence; and he means that, by telling them the reason, he will forestall
their disclosure of it.—*Moult* is an old word used especially of birds when casting their
feathers. So in Bacon's *Natural History:* "Some birds there be, that upon their *moulting*
do turn colour; as robin-redbreasts, after their moulting, grow red again by degrees."

²⁶³ Here, as often, *brave* is *grand, splendid.*

ROSENCRANTZ. To think, my lord, if you delight not in man, what lenten entertainment[264] the players shall receive from you. We coted[265] them on the way; and hither are they coming, to offer you service.

HAMLET. He that plays the king shall be welcome; his majesty shall have tribute of me; the adventurous knight shall use his foil and target; the lover shall not sigh gratis; the humorous[266] man shall end his part in peace; the clown shall make those laugh whose lungs are tickled o' the sear;[267] and the lady shall say her mind freely, or the blank verse shall halt for't.[268] What players are they?

ROSENCRANTZ. Even those you were wont to take delight in, the tragedians of the city.

HAMLET. How chances it they travel? Their residence, both in reputation and profit, was better both ways.[269]

ROSENCRANTZ. I think their inhibition comes by the means of the late inhibition.[270]

HAMLET. Do they hold the same estimation they did when I was in the city? are they so followed?

ROSENCRANTZ. No, indeed, are they not.

HAMLET. How comes it? do they grow rusty?

---

[264] "*Lenten* entertainment" is entertainment for the season of *Lent*, when players were not allowed to perform in public, in London.

[265] To *cote* is, properly, to *overpass*, to *outstrip*. So Scott, in *Old Mortality*, note J.: "This horse was so fleet, and its rider so expert, that they are said to have outstripped and *coted*, or turned, a hare upon the Bran-Law."

[266] *Humorous man* here means a man made unhappy by his own crotchets. *Humour* was used for any wayward, eccentric impulse causing a man to be full of ups and downs, or of flats and sharps. The melancholy Jaques in *As You Like It* is an instance.

[267] *Tickle* is *delicate, sensitive, easily moved. Sear* is the catch of a gunlock, that holds the hammer cocked or half-cocked. Here *o'*, that is, *of*, is equivalent to *in respect of*. The image is of a gunlock with the hammer held so lightly by the catch as to go off at the slightest pressure on the trigger; and the general idea is of persons so prone to laughter, that the least touch or gleam of wit is enough to make them explode. The same thought occurs in *The Tempest*, ii. 1: "I did it to minister occasion to these gentlemen, who are of such *sensible* and nimble lungs, that they always use to laugh at nothing." Here, as in many other places, *sensible* is *sensitive*. In the text, Hamlet is slurring the extemporized witticisms of the Clowns, by a sort of ironical praise. For this explanation I am indebted to the "Clarendon Press Series," which quotes from Howard's *Defensative against the Poyson of supposed Prophecies*, 1620: "Discovering the moods and humors of the vulgar sort to be so loose and *tickle of the seare*."

[268] That is, the poet's feet shall go lame from her overworking them.

[269] The London theatrical companies, when not allowed to play in the city, were wont to travel about the country, and play in the towns. This was less reputable, and also brought less pay, than playing in the city.

[270] Referring, no doubt, to an order of the Privy Council, June, 1600. By this order the players were *inhibited* from acting in or near the city during the season of Lent, besides being very much restricted at all other seasons, and hence "chances it they travel," or *stroll* into the country.

ROSENCRANTZ. Nay, their endeavour keeps in the wonted pace: but
there is, sir, an eyrie of children, little eyases,[271] that cry out on the
top of question,[272] and are most tyrannically clapped for't. These
are now the fashion, and so berattle[273] the common stages—so they
call them—that many wearing rapiers are afraid of goose-quills
and dare scarce come thither.[274]

HAMLET. What, are they children? Who maintains 'em? How are they
escoted?[275] Will they pursue the quality no longer than they can
sing? will they not say afterwards, if they should grow themselves
to common players—as it is most like, if their means are no
better—their writers do them wrong, to make them exclaim against
their own succession?[276]

ROSENCRANTZ. Faith, there has been much to do on both sides; and
the nation holds it no sin to tarre[277] them to controversy: there was,
for a while, no money bid for argument, unless the poet and the
player went to cuffs in the question.[278]

---

[271] *Eyrie*, from *eyren*, eggs, properly means a *brood*, but sometimes a *nest*. *Eyases*
are unfledged hawks.

[272] "Cry out on the top of question" means, I have no doubt, *exclaim against those
who are at the top of their profession*, who are most talked about as having surpassed all
others. Shakespeare uses *cry out on*, or cry *on*, nearly if not quite always in the sense of
exclaim against, or *cry down*. He also often uses *top*, both noun and verb, in the sense of
to *excel* or *surpass*. He also has *question* repeatedly in the sense of *talk* or
conversation.—For this explanation I am mainly indebted to Mr. Joseph Crosby, who
remarks to me upon the whole sentence as follows: "A brood of young hawks, unfledged
nestlings, that exclaim against, or lampoon, the best productions of the dramatic pen;
little chits, that declaim squibs, and turn to ridicule their seniors and betters, both actors
and authors, and are vociferously applauded for it."

[273] To *berattle* is to *berate*, to *squib*. Here, again, I quote from Mr. Crosby: "It is no
wonder the regular profession suffer, when children thus 'carry it away,' and are all 'the
fashion'; berating the adult performers, and getting 'most tyrannically clapp'd for it'; so
much so, that the well-deserving writers for the 'common stages,' grown-up men
'wearing rapiers, are afraid of goose-quills,' (applied to the penny-a-liners for the boys,)
and dare scarce come to the play-house any more."

[274] The allusion is to the children of St. Paul's and of the Revels, whose performing
of plays was much in fashion at the time this play was written. From an early date, the
choir-boys of St. Paul's, Westminster, Windsor, and the Chapel Royal, were engaged in
such performances, and sometimes played at Court. The complaint here is, that these
juveniles abuse "the common stages," that is, the public theatres.

[275] *Escoted is paid*; from the French *escot*, a *shot* or *reckoning.*—*Quality* is
profession or *calling*; often so used.—"No longer than they can sing" means no longer
than they keep the voices of boys.

[276] *Run down* the profession to which they are themselves to *succeed*. This fully
accords with, and approves, the explanation given in note 272. As Mr. Crosby observes,
"it appears that a contest was waging between the patrons of these boy-players, who
wrote their parts for them, and the writers for 'the common stages,' whom the children so
berated and disparaged."

[277] The Poet has *to-do* repeatedly in the exact sense of *ado.*—To *tarre* is to *set on*, to
incite; a word borrowed from the setting-on of dogs.

[278] Not "unless the poet and the player" went to fighting each other, but unless *both*
the *writers* and the *actors* joined together in pelting and running down the full-grown

HAMLET. Is't possible?

GUILDENSTERN. O, there has been much throwing about of brains.[279]

HAMLET. Do the boys carry it away?[280]

ROSENCRANTZ. Ay, that they do, my lord; Hercules and his load too.

HAMLET. It is not very strange; for mine uncle is king of Denmark, and those that would make mows at him while my father lived, give twenty, forty, fifty, an hundred ducats a-piece for his picture in little. 'Sblood, there is something in this more than natural, if philosophy could find it out.

[Flourish of trumpets within.]

GUILDENSTERN. There are the players.

HAMLET. Gentlemen, you are welcome to Elsinore. Your hands, come then: the appurtenance of welcome is fashion and ceremony: let me comply with you in this garb,[281] lest my extent to the players, which, I tell you, must show fairly outward, should more appear like entertainment than yours. You are welcome: but my uncle-father and aunt-mother are deceived.

GUILDENSTERN. In what, my dear lord?

HAMLET. I am but mad north-north-west: when the wind is southerly I know a hawk from a handsaw.[282]

---

regular performers. Here, as often, *argument* is the subject-matter or plot of a play, and so is put for the play itself. *Question*, again, is, apparently, the *dialogue*. So that the meaning of the whole seems to be, "The public would not patronize these juvenile performances, unless both the 'eyases' and the 'goosequills,' (that is, the boy-actors and their writers,) in their dialogue, went to abusing or berating the authors and actors of the 'common stages.'"—CROSBY.

[279] Bandying of wit, or pelting each other with words.

[280] Carry all the world before them: perhaps an allusion to the *Globe* theatre, the sign of which is said to have been Hercules carrying a globe.

[281] To *comply with*, as here used, evidently means to be *formally civil* or *polite to*, or to *compliment*. We have it again in the same sense, in v. 2, where Hamlet says of Osric, "He did *comply with* his dug before he suck'd it."—*Appurtenance* is *appertainings*, or *proper appendages.*—*Garb* is *style* or *manner.* Repeatedly so.—"My *extent* to the players" means *extension* of courtesy and civility to them.

[282] "To know a hawk from a handsaw" was an old proverb. It appears that *handsaw* was a corruption of *hernsew*, meaning what we call *heron.* Probably our best explanation of the text is from Mr. J. C. Heath, as quoted by Mr. Furness in his *Variorum*: "The expression obviously refers to the sport of hawking. Most birds, especially one of heavy flight like the heron, when roused by the falconer or his dog, would fly down or with the wind, in order to escape. When the wind is from the North, the heron flies towards the South; and the spectator may be dazzled by the Sun, and be unable to distinguish the hawk from the heron. On the other hand, when the wind is southerly, the heron flies towards the North, and it and the pursuing hawk are clearly seen by the sportsman, who then has his back to the Sun, and without difficulty knows the hawk from the hernsew. A curious reader may further observe that a wind from the precise point north-north-west

[*Enter* POLONIUS.]

POLONIUS. Well be with you, gentlemen!

HAMLET. Hark you, Guildenstern; and you too: at each ear a hearer: that great baby you see there is not yet out of his swaddling-clouts.

ROSENCRANTZ. Happily he's the second time come to them; for they say an old man is twice a child.

HAMLET. I will prophesy he comes to tell me of the players; mark it. You say right, sir: o' Monday morning; 'twas so indeed.[283]

POLONIUS. My lord, I have news to tell you.

HAMLET. My lord, I have news to tell you. When Roscius was an actor in Rome—

POLONIUS. The actors are come hither, my lord.

HAMLET. Buzz, buzz![284]

POLONIUS. Upon mine honour—

HAMLET. Then came each actor on his ass—

POLONIUS. The best actors in the world, either for tragedy, comedy, history, pastoral, pastoral-comical, historical-pastoral, tragical-historical, tragical-comical-historical-pastoral, scene individable, or poem unlimited:[285] Seneca cannot be too heavy, nor Plautus too light. For the law of writ and the liberty,[286] these are the only men.

HAMLET. O Jephthah, judge of Israel, what a treasure hadst thou!

POLONIUS. What a treasure had he, my lord?

HAMLET. Why—
    'One fair daughter and no more,
    The which he loved passing well.'

POLONIUS. [*Aside.*] Still on my daughter.

HAMLET. Am I not i' the right, old Jephthah?

---

would be in the eye of the Sun at half-past ten in the forenoon, a likely time for hawking, whereas *southerly* includes a wider range of wind for a good view."

[283] This is spoken, apparently, in order to blind Polonius as to what they have been talking about.

[284] Hamlet affects to discredit the news: all a mere *buzzing* or *rumour*. Polonius then assures him, "On my honour"; which starts the poor joke, "If they are come on your honour, 'then came each actor on his ass'"; these latter words being probably a quotation from some ballad.

[285] *Individable* for *undivided.* The Poet has many like instances of the endings *-able* or *-idle* and *-ed* used indiscriminately. In the text, *scene* and *poem* are evidently used as equivalent terms. In the Greek Tragedy there was no division into scenes; the scene continued the same, or *undivided*, all through the piece. But in the Gothic Drama, as Shakespeare found and fixed it, the changes of scene are without definite limitations. This seems to be the difference meant. Seneca was considered the best of the Roman tragic writers, and Plautus of the comic.

[286] "The meaning," says Collier, "probably is, that the players were good, whether at written productions or at extemporal plays, where liberty was allowed to the performers to invent the dialogue, in imitation of the Italian *commedie al improviso*."

POLONIUS. If you call me Jephthah, my lord, I have a daughter that I love passing well.

HAMLET. Nay, that follows not.

POLONIUS. What follows, then, my lord?

HAMLET. Why—

'As by lot, God wot,'

and then, you know,

'It came to pass, as most like it was,[287]'—

The first row of the pious chanson[288] will show you more; for look, where my abridgement comes.[289]

[*Enter the Players.*]

You are welcome, masters; welcome, all.—I am glad to see thee well. Welcome, good friends. O, my old friend! thy face is valenc'd since I saw thee last:[290] com'st thou to beard me in Denmark? What, my young lady and mistress! By'r lady,[291] your ladyship is nearer to heaven than when I saw you last, by the altitude of a chopine.[292] Pray God, your voice, like apiece of

---

[287] Hamlet is teasing the old fox, and quibbling between a logical and a literal sequence. The lines he quotes are from an old ballad, entitled Jephtha, *Judge of Israel*. A copy of the ballad, as Shakespeare knew it, was reprinted in Evan's *Old Ballads*, 1810; the first stanza as follows:

> I have read that many years agoe,
> When Jephtha, judge of Israel,
> Had one fair daughter and no moe,
> Whom he loved passing well;
>   As by lot, God wot,
>   It came to passe, most like it was,
> Great warrs there should be,
> And who should be the chiefe but he, but he.

[288] *Chanson* is something to be *sung* or *chanted*; and "the first *row*" probably means the first *column*, or, perhaps, *stanza*.

[289] Perhaps Hamlet calls the players "my *abridgements*" in the same sense and for the same reason as he afterwards calls them "the abstracts and brief chronicles of the time." He may have the further meaning of *abridging* or *cutting short* his talk with Polonius. Or, again, he may mean that their office is to *abridge the time*, or to minister *pastimes*.

[290] *Valanced* is *fringed*. The player has lately grown a beard.

[291] *By'r Lady* is a contraction of *by our Lady*, referring to the Virgin Mary. In the Poet's time, female parts were acted by boys; and Hamlet is addressing one whom as a boy he had seen playing some heroine.

[292] *Chopine* was the name of an enormously thick-soled shoe which Spanish and

uncurrent gold, be not cracked within the ring.[293] Masters, you are
all welcome. We'll e'en to't like French falconers, fly at any thing
we see:[294] we'll have a speech straight: come, give us a taste of
your quality; come, a passionate speech.

FIRST PLAYER. What speech, my lord?

HAMLET. I heard thee speak me a speech once, but it was never acted;
or, if it was, not above once; for the play, I remember, pleased not
the million; 'twas caviar to the general:[295] but it was—as I received
it, and others, whose judgments in such matters cried in the top of
mine[296]—an excellent play, well digested in the scenes, set down
with as much modesty as cunning. I remember, one said there were
no sallets in the lines to make the matter savoury,[297] nor no matter
in the phrase that might indict the author of affectation; but called
it an honest method, as wholesome as sweet, and by very much
more handsome than fine. One speech in it I chiefly loved: 'twas
Aeneas' tale to Dido; and thereabout of it especially, where he
speaks of Priam's slaughter: if it live in your memory, begin at this
line: let me see, let me see:

'The rugged Pyrrhus, like the Hyrcanian beast,'

'Tis not so:—it begins with Pyrrhus.

'The rugged Pyrrhus, he whose sable arms,
Black as his purpose, did the night resemble
When he lay couched in the ominous horse,
Hath now this dread and black complexion smear'd
With heraldry more dismal; head to foot

Italian ladies were in the habit of wearing, in order, as would seem, to make themselves
as tall as the men, perhaps taller; or it may have been, to keep their long skirts from
mopping the sidewalks too much. The fashion is said to have been used at one time by
the English.

[293] The old gold coin was thin and liable to crack. There was a *ring* or circle on it,
within which the sovereign's head was stamped; if the crack extended beyond this ring, it
was rendered uncurrent: it was therefore a simile applied to any other injured object.
There *is* some humour in applying it to *a cracked voice.*

[294] From this it would seem that the English custom in falconry was, first to let off
some bird into the air, and then to fly the hawk after it; the French, to fly the hawk at any
bird that might happen to be within ken.

[295] *Caviar* was the pickled roes of certain fish of the sturgeon kind, called in Italy
caviale, and much used there and in other countries. Great quantities were prepared on
the river Volga formerly. As a dish of high seasoning and peculiar flavour, it was not
relished by the *many.*

[296] Meaning, probably, were *better than mine.*

[297] No impertinent high-seasoning or false brilliancy, to give it an unnatural relish.
Sallet is explained "a pleasant and merry word that maketh folk to laugh."—This passage
shows that the Poet understood the essential poverty of "fine writing."

Now is he total gules;[298] horridly trick'd
With blood of fathers, mothers, daughters, sons,
Baked and impasted with the parching streets,
That lend a tyrannous and damned light
To their lord's murder: roasted in wrath and fire,
And thus o'er-sized with coagulate gore,
With eyes like carbuncles, the hellish Pyrrhus
Old grandsire Priam seeks.'

So, proceed you.
POLONIUS. 'Fore God, my lord, well spoken, with good accent and
good discretion.
FIRST PLAYER. 'Anon he finds him
Striking too short at Greeks; his antique sword,
Rebellious to his arm, lies where it falls,
Repugnant to command: unequal match'd,
Pyrrhus at Priam drives; in rage strikes wide;
But with the whiff and wind of his fell sword
The unnerved father falls. Then senseless Ilium,
Seeming to feel this blow, with flaming top
Stoops to his base, and with a hideous crash
Takes prisoner Pyrrhus' ear: for, lo! his sword,
Which was declining on the milky head
Of reverend Priam, seem'd i' the air to stick:
So, as a painted tyrant, Pyrrhus stood,
And like a neutral to his will and matter,
Did nothing.
But, as we often see, against some storm,
A silence in the heavens, the rack[299] stand still,
The bold winds speechless and the orb below
As hush as death, anon the dreadful thunder
Doth rend the region,[300] so, after Pyrrhus' pause,
Aroused vengeance sets him new a-work;
And never did the Cyclops' hammers fall
On Mars's armour forged for proof eterne[301]
With less remorse than Pyrrhus' bleeding sword
Now falls on Priam.—

---

[298] *Gules* is *red*, in the language of heraldry: to *trick* is to colour.

[299] *Rack*, from reek, is used by old writers to signify the highest and therefore lightest clouds. So in Fletcher's *Women Pleased*, iv. 2: "Far swifter than the sailing *rack* that gallops upon the wings of angry winds." So that the heavens must be silent indeed, when "the rack stands still."

[300] *Region*, here, is *sky*, or the *air*. So in the last speech of this scene: "I should have fatted all the *region* kites," &c.

[301] For *eternal resistance* to assault. As we say *shot-proof, water-proof.*

Out, out, thou strumpet, Fortune! All you gods,
In general synod 'take away her power;
Break all the spokes and fellies from her wheel,
And bowl the round nave down the hill of heaven,
As low as to the fiends!'
POLONIUS. This is too long.
HAMLET. It shall to the barber's, with your beard. Prithee, say on: he's for a jig[302] or a tale of bawdry, or he sleeps: say on: come to Hecuba.
FIRST PLAYER. 'But who, O, who had seen the mobled queen—'
HAMLET. 'The mobled queen?'
POLONIUS. That's good; 'mobled queen' is good.[303]
FIRST PLAYER. 'Run barefoot up and down, threatening the flames
With bisson rheum;[304] a clout upon that head
Where late the diadem stood, and for a robe,
About her lank and all o'er-teemed loins,
A blanket, in the alarm of fear caught up—
Who this had seen, with tongue in venom steep'd,
'Gainst Fortune's state would treason have pronounced:
But if the gods themselves did see her then
When she saw Pyrrhus make malicious sport
In mincing with his sword her husband's limbs,
The instant burst of clamour that she made,
Unless things mortal move them not at all,
Would have made milch the burning eyes of heaven,
And passion in the gods.'[305]
POLONIUS. Look, whether he has not turned his colour and has tears in's eyes. Pray you, no more.
HAMLET. 'Tis well: I'll have thee speak out the rest soon. Good my lord, will you see the players well bestowed? Do you hear, let them be well used; for they are the abstract and brief chronicles of the time:[306] after your death you were better have a bad epitaph than their ill report while you live.
POLONIUS. My lord, I will use them according to their desert.

---

[302] *Giga*, in Italian, was a fiddle or crowd; *gigaro*, a fiddler, or minstrel. Hence *a jig* was a ballad, or ditty, sung to the fiddle.

[303] *Mobled* is *hastily* or *carelessly dressed.* To *mob* or *mab* is still used in the north of England for to dress in a slatternly manner; and Coleridge says "*mob-cap* is still a word in common use for a morning cap."

[304] *Bisson* is *blind. Bisson rheum* is therefore *blinding tears.*—A *clout* is simply a piece of cloth or of linen.

[305] By a hardy poetical license this expression means, "Would have *filled with tears* the burning eyes of heaven."—*Passion*, here, is *compassion.*

[306] The condensed efficacies and representatives of the age. In Shakespeare's time, the Drama, including both authors and actors, was a sort of Fourth Estate; perhaps as much so as the Newspaper is now.

HAMLET. God's bodykins,[307] man, much better: use every man after his desert, and who should 'scape whipping? Use them after your own honour and dignity: the less they deserve, the more merit is in your bounty. Take them in.
POLONIUS. Come, sirs.
HAMLET. Follow him, friends: we'll hear a play to-morrow. Dost thou hear me, old friend; can you play the Murder of Gonzago?
FIRST PLAYER. Ay, my lord.
HAMLET. We'll ha't to-morrow night. You could, for a need, study a speech of some dozen or sixteen lines, which I would set down and insert in't, could you not?
FIRST PLAYER. Ay, my lord.
HAMLET. Very well. Follow that lord; and look you mock him not. [*Exit* FIRST PLAYER.] My good friends, I'll leave you till night: you are welcome to Elsinore.
ROSENCRANTZ. Good my lord!
HAMLET. Ay, so, God buy to you!

[*Exeunt* ROSENCRANTZ *and* GUILDENSTERN.]

Now I am alone.
O, what a rogue and peasant slave am I!
Is it not monstrous that this player here,
But in a fiction, in a dream of passion,
Could force his soul so to his own conceit
That from her working all his visage wann'd;
Tears in his eyes, distraction in's aspect,
A broken voice, and his whole function suiting
With forms to his conceit?[308] and all for nothing!
For Hecuba!
What's Hecuba to him, or he to Hecuba,
That he should weep for her? What would he do,
Had he the motive and the cue[309] for passion
That I have? He would drown the stage with tears
And cleave the general ear with horrid speech,
Make mad the guilty and appall the free,
Confound the ignorant, and amaze indeed
The very faculties of eyes and ears. Yet I,
A dull and muddy-mettl'd rascal, peak,
Like John-a-dreams,[310] unpregnant of my cause,

[307] *Bodykins* is merely a diminutive of *body*.

[308] *Conceit* is used by the Poet for *conception* or *imagination*.

[309] The *hint* or *prompt-word.* "A prompter," says Florio, "one who keepes the booke for the plaiers, and teacheth them their *kue.*"

[310] This John was probably distinguished as a sort of dreaming or droning simpleton

And can say nothing; no, not for a king,
Upon whose property and most dear life
A damn'd defeat was made. Am I a coward?
Who calls me villain? breaks my pate across?
Plucks off my beard, and blows it in my face?
Tweaks me by the nose? gives me the lie i' the throat,
As deep as to the lungs?[311] who does me this, ha?
'Swounds, I should take it: for it cannot be
But I am pigeon-liver'd and lack gall
To make oppression bitter,[312] or ere this
I should have fatted all the region kites[313]
With this slave's offal: bloody, bawdy villain!
Remorseless, treacherous, lecherous, kindless[314] villain!
O, vengeance!—
Why, what an ass am I! This is most brave,
That I, the son of a dear father murder'd,
Prompted to my revenge by heaven and hell,[315]
Must, like a whore, unpack my heart with words,
And fall a-cursing, like a very drab, A scullion!
Fie upon't! foh! About, my brain![316] I have heard
That guilty creatures sitting at a play
Have by the very cunning of the scene
Been struck so to the soul that presently
They have proclaim'd their malefactions;
For murder, though it have no tongue, will speak
With most miraculous organ. I'll have these players
Play something like the murder of my father
Before mine uncle: I'll observe his looks;
I'll tent him to the quick: if he but blench,[317]
I know my course. The spirit that I have seen
May be the devil: and the devil hath power

---

or flunky, or, perhaps, merely an apathetic, sleepy fellow. The only other mention of him that has reached us is in Armin's *Nest of Ninnies*, 1608: "His name is John, indeed, says the cinnick, but neither John a-nods nor *John a-dreams*, yet either, as you take it."

[311] This was giving one the lie with the most galling additions and terms of insult; so that the not resenting it would stamp him as the most hopeless of cowards.

[312] "Lack gall to make me feel the bitterness of oppression"; or, perhaps, to make oppression bitter to the oppressor.—The gentleness of doves and pigeons were supposed to proceed from their having no gall in them.

[313] All the kites of the *airy* region, the sky.

[314] *Kindless* is *unnatural*.—Observe how Hamlet checks himself in this strain of objurgation, and then, in mere shame of what he has just done, turns to ranting at himself for having ranted.

[315] By all the best and all the worst passions of his nature.

[316] "*About*, my brain," is nothing more than "*to work*, my brain." The phrase to go *about* a thing, is still common.

[317] To *tent* was to *probe* a wound. To *blench* is to *shrink* or *start.*

To assume a pleasing shape; yea, and perhaps
Out of my weakness and my melancholy,
As he is very potent with such spirits,
Abuses me to damn me:[318] I'll have grounds
More relative than this:[319] the play's the thing
Wherein I'll catch the conscience of the king. [*Exit.*]

---

[318] Hamlet was not alone in the suspicion here started. Sir Thomas Browne, *Religio Medici*: "I believe that those apparitions and ghosts of departed persons are not the wandering souls of men, but the unquiet walks of devils, prompting and suggesting us into mischief, blood, and villainy; instilling and stealing into our hearts that the blessed spirits are not at rest in their graves, but wander, solicitous of the affairs of the world."— To *abuse* is to *deceive*, or *practise upon* with illusions.

[319] Grounds standing in closer and clearer relation with the matter alleged by the Ghost.

ACT III.

SCENE I.

Elsinore. A Room in the Castle.

[*Enter the* KING, *the* QUEEN, POLONIUS, OPHELIA,
ROSENCRANTZ, *and* GUILDENSTERN.]

KING. And can you, by no drift of circumstance,[320]
    Get from him why he puts on this confusion,
    Grating so harshly all his days of quiet
    With turbulent and dangerous lunacy?
ROSENCRANTZ. He does confess he feels himself distracted;
    But from what cause he will by no means speak.
GUILDENSTERN. Nor do we find him forward to be sounded,
    But, with a crafty madness, keeps aloof,
    When we would bring him on to some confession
    Of his true state.
QUEEN. Did he receive you well?
ROSENCRANTZ. Most like a gentleman.
GUILDENSTERN. But with much forcing of his disposition.
ROSENCRANTZ. Niggard of question;[321] but, of our demands,
    Most free in his reply.
QUEEN. Did you assay him?
    To any pastime?
ROSENCRANTZ. Madam, it so fell out, that certain players
    We o'er-raught[322] on the way: of these we told him;
    And there did seem in him a kind of joy
    To hear of it: they are about the court,
    And, as I think, they have already order
    This night to play before him.
POLONIUS. 'Tis most true:
    And he beseech'd me to entreat your majesties
    To hear and see the matter.
KING. With all my heart; and it doth much content me
    To hear him so inclined.
    Good gentlemen, give him a further edge,
    And drive his purpose on to these delights.

---

[320] Course of indirect, roundabout inquiry.
[321] Here, *of* is equivalent to *in respect of.* Also in "*of* our demands." *Question* may mean *inquiry,* or *conversation;* and either of these senses accords with the occasion referred to.
[322] *O'er-raught* is *overtook; raught* being an old form of *reached.*

ROSENCRANTZ. We shall, my lord.

[*Exeunt* ROSENCRANTZ *and* GUIDENSTERN.]

KING. Sweet Gertrude, leave us too;
    For we have closely[323] sent for Hamlet hither,
    That he, as 'twere by accident, may here
    Affront[324] Ophelia:
    Her father and myself, lawful espials,
    Will so bestow ourselves that, seeing, unseen,
    We may of their encounter frankly judge,
    And gather by him, as he is behaved,
    If't be the affliction of his love or no
    That thus he suffers for.
QUEEN. I shall obey you.
    And for your part, Ophelia, I do wish
    That your good beauties be the happy cause
    Of Hamlet's wildness: so shall I hope your virtues
    Will bring him to his wonted way again,
    To both your honours.
OPHELIA. Madam, I wish it may. [*Exit* QUEEN.]
POLONIUS. Ophelia, walk you here. Gracious, so please you,
    We will bestow ourselves.—[*To* OPHELIA.] Read on this book;
    That show of such an exercise may colour
    Your loneliness. We are oft to blame in this:
    'Tis too much proved, that with devotion's visage
    And pious action we do sugar o'er
    The devil himself.
KING. [*Aside.*] O, 'tis too true!
    How smart a lash that speech doth give my conscience!
    The harlot's cheek, beautied with plastering art,
    Is not more ugly[325] to the thing that helps it
    Than is my deed to my most painted word:
    O heavy burthen!
POLONIUS. I hear him coming: let's withdraw, my lord.

[*Exeunt* KING *and* POLONIUS.]

[*Enter* HAMLET.]

---

[323] *Closely* is *secretly*; sent in such a way as not to let Hamlet know from whom the message came: a *got-up* accident.

[324] *Affront* was sometimes used for *meet*, or, as it is explained a little after, *encounter*. So in Cymbeline, iv. 3: "Your preparation can *affront* no less than what you hear of."

[325] Not more ugly *in comparison with* the things that helps it.

HAMLET. To be, or not to be: that is the question:
    Whether 'tis nobler in the mind to suffer
    The slings and arrows of outrageous fortune,
    Or to take arms against a sea of troubles,
    And by opposing end them? To die: to sleep;
    No more; and by a sleep to say we end
    The heart-ache and the thousand natural shocks
    That flesh is heir to, 'tis a consummation
    Devoutly to be wish'd. To die, to sleep;
    To sleep: perchance to dream: ay, there's the rub;[326]
    For in that sleep of death what dreams may come
    When we have shuffled off this mortal coil,[327]
    Must give us pause: there's the respect
    That makes calamity of so long life;[328]
    For who would bear the whips and scorns of time,
    The oppressor's wrong, the proud man's contumely,
    The pangs of despised love, the law's delay,
    The insolence of office and the spurns
    That patient merit of the unworthy takes,
    When he himself might his quietus[329] make
    With a bare bodkin? who would fardels[330] bear,
    To grunt and sweat under a weary life,
    But that the dread of something after death,
    The undiscover'd country from whose bourn
    No traveller returns,[331] puzzles the will
    And makes us rather bear those ills we have
    Than fly to others that we know not of?
    Thus conscience does make cowards of us all;
    And thus the native hue of resolution
    Is sicklied o'er with the pale cast of thought,[332]

---

[326] *Rub* is *obstruction, hindrance.* A word borrowed from the bowling alley, where it was used of any thing that deflected the bowl from its aim.

[327] "This mortal *coil*" is the tumult and bustle of this mortal life; or, as Wordsworth has it, "the fretful stir unprofitable, and the fever of the world." Perhaps *coil* here means, also, the body.

[328] That is, the *consideration* that induces us to undergo the calamity of so long a life. This use of *respect* is very frequent.

[329] The allusion is to the term *quietus est,* used in settling accounts at exchequer audits. So in Sir Thomas Overbury's character of *a Franklin:* "Lastly, to *end* him, he cares not when his end comes; he needs not feare his audit, for his *quietus* is in heaven."—*Bodkin* was the ancient term for a small dagger.

[330] *Fardel* is an old word for *burden* or *bundle.*

[331] *Bourn* is *boundary.* So in *Troilus and Cressida,* ii. 3: "I will not praise thy wisdom, which, like a *bourn,* a pale, a shore, confines thy spacious and dilated parts."— Of course Hamlet means that, as Coleridge says, "no traveller returns to this world as his home or abiding-place."

And enterprises of great pith and moment
With this regard their currents turn awry,
And lose the name of action.—Soft you now!
The fair Ophelia! Nymph, in thy orisons
Be all my sins rememb'red.

OPHELIA. Good my lord,
How does your honour for this many a day?

HAMLET. I humbly thank you; well, well, well.

OPHELIA. My lord, I have remembrances of yours,
That I have longed long to re-deliver;
I pray you, now receive them.

HAMLET. No, not I;
I never gave you aught.

OPHELIA. My honour'd lord, you know right well you did;
And, with them, words of so sweet breath composed
As made the things more rich: their perfume lost,
Take these again; for to the noble mind
Rich gifts wax poor when givers prove unkind.
There, my lord.

HAMLET. Ha, ha! are you honest?

OPHELIA. My lord?

HAMLET. Are you fair?

OPHELIA. What means your lordship?

HAMLET. That if you be honest and fair, your honesty should admit no discourse to your beauty.[333]

OPHELIA. Could beauty, my lord, have better commerce than with honesty?

HAMLET. Ay, truly; for the power of beauty will sooner transform honesty from what it is to a bawd than the force of honesty can translate beauty into his likeness: this was sometime a paradox, but now the time gives it proof. I did love you once.

OPHELIA. Indeed, my lord, you made me believe so.

HAMLET. You should not have believed me; for virtue cannot so inoculate our old stock but we shall relish of it:[334] I loved you not.

OPHELIA. I was the more deceived.

HAMLET. Get thee to a nunnery: why wouldst thou be a breeder of sinners? I am myself indifferent honest;[335] but yet I could accuse

---

[332] That is, the pale *complexion of grief. Thought* was often used in this way. So in *Twelfth Night*, ii. 4: "She pined *in thought*"; that is, she wasted away *through grief.*

[333] "Your *chastity* should have no conversation or acquaintance with your beauty." This use of *honesty* for *chastity* is very frequent in Shakespeare.—It should be noted, that in these speeches Hamlet refers, not to Ophelia personally, but to the sex in general. So, especially, when he says, "I have heard of your paintings too," he does not mean that Ophelia paints, but that the use of painting is common with her sex.

[334] "Cannot so penetrate and purify our nature, but that we shall still have a strong taste of our native badness."

me of such things that it were better my mother had not borne me:
I am very proud, revengeful, ambitious, with more offences at my
beck[336] than I have thoughts to put them in, imagination to give
them shape, or time to act them in. What should such fellows as I
do crawling between earth and heaven? We are arrant knaves, all;
believe none of us. Go thy ways to a nunnery. Where's your
father?

OPHELIA. At home, my lord.

HAMLET. Let the doors be shut upon him, that he may play the fool
no where but in's own house. Farewell.

OPHELIA. [*Aside.*] O, help him, you sweet heavens!

HAMLET. If thou dost marry, I'll give thee this plague for thy dowry:
be thou as chaste as ice, as pure as snow, thou shalt not escape
calumny. Get thee to a nunnery, go: farewell. Or, if thou wilt needs
marry, marry a fool; for wise men know well enough what
monsters you make of them. To a nunnery, go, and quickly too.
Farewell.

OPHELIA. [*Aside.*] O heavenly powers, restore him!

HAMLET. I have heard of your paintings too, well enough; God has
given you one face, and you make yourselves another: you jig, you
amble, and you lisp, and nick-name God's creatures, and make
your wantonness your ignorance.[337] Go to, I'll no more on't; it hath
made me mad. I say, we will have no more marriages: those that
are married already, all but one, shall live; the rest shall keep as
they are. To a nunnery, go.[338] [*Exit.*]

OPHELIA. O, what a noble mind is here o'er-thrown!
    The courtier's, soldier's, scholar's, eye, tongue, sword;
    The expectancy and rose of the fair state,
    The glass of fashion and the mould of form,[339]
    The observed of all observers, quite, quite down!

---

[335] "*Indifferent* honest" is *tolerably* honest.

[336] That is, "ready to come about me on a signal of permission."

[337] Johnson explains this, "You mistake by wanton affectation, and pretend to
mistake by *ignorance.*" Moberly, "You use ambiguous words, as if you did not know
their meaning."

[338] Throughout the latter part of this fine scene, Hamlet's disorder runs to a very
high pitch, and he seems to take an insane delight in lacerating the gentle creature before
him. Yet what keenness and volubility of wit! what energy and swiftness of discourse!
the intellectual forces in a fiery gallop, while the social feelings seem totally benumbed.
And when Ophelia meets his question, "Where's your father?" with the reply, "At home,
my lord," how quickly he darts upon the true meaning of her presence! The sweet,
innocent girl, who knows not how to word an untruth, having never tried on a lie in her
life, becomes embarrassed in her part; and from her manner Hamlet instantly gathers
what is on foot, and forthwith shapes his speech so as to sting the eavesdroppers.

[339] This is well explained in what Lady Percy says of her lost Hotspur, in *2 King
Henry IV.*, ii. 3: "By his light did all the chivalry of England move; he was indeed the
glass wherein the noble youth did dress themselves."

And I, of ladies most deject and wretched,
That suck'd the honey of his music vows,
Now see that noble and most sovereign reason,
Like sweet bells jangled, out of tune and harsh;
That unmatch'd form and feature of blown youth
Blasted with ecstasy: O, woe is me,
To have seen what I have seen, see what I see!

[*Re-enter* KING *and* POLONIUS.]

KING. Love! his affections do not that way tend;
　　Nor what he spake, though it lack'd form a little,
　　Was not like madness. There's something in his soul,
　　O'er which his melancholy sits on brood;
　　And I do doubt the hatch and the disclose
　　Will be some danger: which for to prevent,
　　I have in quick determination
　　Thus set it down: he shall with speed to England,
　　For the demand of our neglected tribute
　　Haply the seas and countries different
　　With variable objects shall expel
　　This something-settled matter in his heart,
　　Whereon his brains still beating puts him thus
　　From fashion of himself. What think you on't?
POLONIUS. It shall do well: but yet do I believe
　　The origin and commencement of his grief
　　Sprung from neglected love. How now, Ophelia!
　　You need not tell us what Lord Hamlet said;
　　We heard it all. My lord, do as you please;
　　But, if you hold it fit, after the play
　　Let his queen mother all alone entreat him
　　To show his grief: let her be round with him;
　　And I'll be placed, so please you, in the ear
　　Of all their conference. If she find him not,
　　To England send him, or confine him where
　　Your wisdom best shall think.
KING. It shall be so:
　　Madness in great ones must not unwatch'd go. [*Exeunt.*]

SCENE II.

The Same. A Hall in the Castle.

[*Enter* HAMLET *and several Players.*][340]

HAMLET. Speak the speech, I pray you, as I pronounced it to you, trippingly on the tongue: but if you mouth it, as many of your players do, I had as lief the town-crier spoke my lines. Nor do not saw the air too much with your hand, thus, but use all gently; for in the very torrent, tempest, and, as I may say, the whirlwind of passion, you must acquire and beget a temperance that may give it smoothness. O, it offends me to the soul to hear a robustious periwig-pated fellow tear a passion to tatters, to very rags, to split the ears of the groundlings,[341] who for the most part are capable of nothing but inexplicable dumb shows and noise: I would have such a fellow whipped for o'erdoing Termagant; it out-herods Herod:[342] pray you, avoid it.

FIRST PLAYER. I warrant your honour.

HAMLET. Be not too tame neither, but let your own discretion be your tutor: suit the action to the word, the word to the action; with this special o'er-step not the modesty of nature: for any thing so overdone is from the purpose of playing, whose end, both at the first and now, was and is, to hold, as 'twere, the mirror up to nature; to show virtue her own feature, scorn her own image, and the very age and body of the time his form and pressure.[343] Now this overdone, or come tardy of, [344] though it make the unskillful laugh, cannot but make the judicious grieve; the censure of the

---

[340] "This dialogue of Hamlet with the players," says Coleridge, "is one of the happiest instances of Shakespeare's power of diversifying the scene while he is carrying on the plot."

[341] The ancient theatres were far from the commodious, elegant structures which later times have seen. The *pit* was, truly, what its name denotes, an unfloored space in the area of the house, sunk considerably beneath the level of the stage. Hence this part of the audience were called *groundlings*.

[342] *Termagant* is the name given in old romances to the tempestuous god of the Saracens. He is usually joined with *Mahound*, or Mahomet. John Florio calls him "*Termigisto*, a great boaster, quarreller, killer, tamer, or ruler of the universe; the child of the earthquake and of the thunder, the brother of death." Hence this personage was introduced into the old Miracle-plays as a demon of outrageous and violent demeanour. The murder of the innocents was a favourite subject for a Miracle-play; and wherever Herod is introduced, he plays the part of a vaunting braggart, a tyrant of tyrants, and does indeed *outdo Termagant.*

[343] *Pressure* is *impression* here; as when, in i. 5: Hamlet says, "I'll wipe away all forms, all *pressures* past."

[344] To "come tardy of" a thing is the same as to come short of it.

which one must in your allowance,[345] o'erweigh a whole theatre of others. O, there be players that I have seen play, and heard others praise, and that highly, not to speak it profanely, that, neither having the accent of Christians nor the gait of Christian, pagan, nor man, have so strutted and bellowed that I have thought some of nature's journeymen had made men and not made them well, they imitated humanity so abominably.

FIRST PLAYER. I hope we have reformed that indifferently with us, sir.

HAMLET. O, reform it altogether. And let those that play your clowns speak no more than is set down for them; for there be of them that will themselves laugh, to set on some quantity of barren spectators to laugh too; though, in the mean time, some necessary question of the play be then to be considered: that's villainous, and shows a most pitiful ambition in the fool that uses it. Go, make you ready. [*Exeunt Players.*]

[*Enter* POLONIUS, ROSENCRANTZ, *and* GUILDENSTERN.]

How now, my lord! I will the king hear this piece of work?

POLONIUS. And the queen too, and that presently.

HAMLET. Bid the players make haste. [*Exit* POLONIUS.]—Will you two help to hasten them?

ROSENCRANTZ. Ay, my lord.

[*Exeunt* ROSENCRANTZ *and* GUILDENSTERN.]

HAMLET. What ho! Horatio!

[*Enter* HORATIO.]

HORATIO. Here, sweet lord, at your service.

HAMLET. Horatio, thou art e'en as just a man
As e'er my conversation coped withal.

HORATIO. O, my dear lord!

HAMLET. Nay, do not think I flatter;
For what advancement may I hope from thee
That no revenue[346] hast but thy good spirits,

---

[345] "The *censure* of the *which one* "means the *judgment* of *one of which*, or of *whom*. This use of *censure* is very frequent.—*Allowance* is *estimation* or *approval*. To *approve* is the more frequent meaning of to *allow*, in Shakespeare. And so in the Bible; as, "The Lord *alloweth* the righteous."

[346] Here, and generally, though not always, in Shakespeare, *revenue* has the accent on the second syllable. And so, I believe, it is uniformly sounded by all the other English poets. So, too, Webster, Choate, and Everett always spoke it.

To feed and clothe thee? Why should the poor be flatter'd?
No, let the candied tongue lick absurd pomp,
And crook the pregnant[347] hinges of the knee
Where thrift may follow fawning. Dost thou hear?
Since my dear soul was mistress of her choice
And could of men distinguish, her election
Hath seal'd thee for herself; for thou hast been
As one, in suffering all, that suffers nothing,
A man that fortune's buffets and rewards
Hast ta'en with equal thanks: and blest are those
Whose blood and judgment are so well commingled,
That they are not a pipe for fortune's finger
To sound what stop she please. Give me that man
That is not passion's slave, and I will wear him
In my heart's core, ay, in my heart of heart,
As I do thee. Something too much of this.
There is a play to-night before the king;
One scene of it comes near the circumstance
Which I have told thee of my father's death:
I prithee, when thou seest that act afoot,
Even with the very comment of thy soul
Observe mine uncle. if his occulted guilt
Do not itself unkennel in one speech,
It is a damned ghost that we have seen,
And my imaginations are as foul
As Vulcan's stithy.[348] Give him heedful note;
For I mine eyes will rivet to his face,
And after we will both our judgments join
In censure of his seeming.
HORATIO. Well, my lord.
If he steal aught the whilst this play is playing,
And 'scape detecting, I will pay the theft.
HAMLET. They are coming to the play; I must be idle:[349] Get you a
place.

[*Danish march. A flourish. Enter the* KING, *the* QUEEN,
POLONIUS, OPHELIA, ROSENCRANTZ,
GUILDENSTERN, *and others.*]

KING. How fares our cousin Hamlet?

---

[347] *Pregnant* is *ready, prompt.—Candied* is *sugared*; a tongue steeped in the
sweetness of adulation.—*Thrift* is *profit*; the gold that flatterers lie for.

[348] Vulcan's workshop or *smithy*; *stith* being an *anvil.*

[349] Must *seem* idle; must behave as if his mind were purposeless, or intent upon
nothing in particular.

HAMLET. Excellent, i' faith; of the chameleon's dish: I eat the air, promise-crammed:[350] you cannot feed capons so.

KING. I have nothing with this answer, Hamlet; these words are not mine.

HAMLET. No, nor mine now. [*To* POLONIUS.] My lord, you played once i' the university, you say?

POLONIUS. That did I, my lord; and was accounted a good actor.

HAMLET. What did you enact?

POLONIUS. I did enact Julius Caesar: I was killed i' the Capitol; Brutus killed me.[351]

HAMLET. It was a brute part of him to kill so capital a calf there.[352] Be the players ready?

ROSENCRANTZ. Ay, my lord; they stay upon your patience.

QUEEN. Come hither, my dear Hamlet, sit by me.

HAMLET. No, good mother, here's metal more attractive.

POLONIUS. [*To the* KING.] O, ho! do you mark that?

HAMLET. Lady, shall I lie in your lap?

[*Lying down at* OPHELIA'*s feet.*]

OPHELIA. No, my lord.

HAMLET. I mean, my head upon your lap?

OPHELIA. Ay, my lord.

HAMLET. Do you think I meant country matters?

OPHELIA. I think nothing, my lord.

HAMLET. That's a fair thought to lie between maids' legs.

OPHELIA. What is, my lord?

HAMLET. Nothing.

OPHELIA. You are merry, my lord.

HAMLET. Who, I?

OPHELIA. Ay, my lord.

HAMLET. O God, your only jig-maker. What should a man do but be merry? for, look you, how cheerfully my mother looks, and my father died within's[353] these two hours.

---

[350] Because the chameleon was supposed to live on air. In fact, this and various other reptiles will live a long time without any visible food. So in *Othello*, iii. 3: "I had rather be a toad, and *live upon the vapour* of a dungeon," *Sec.*—The King snuffs offence in "I eat the air, promise-cramm'd," as implying that he has not kept his promise to Hamlet.

[351] A Latin play on Caesar's death was performed at Christ's Church, Oxford, in 1582. Malone thinks that there was an English play on the same subject previous to Shakespeare's. Caesar was killed in *Pompey's portico*, and not in the Capitol; but the error is at least as old as Chaucer's time.

[352] He *acted* the part of a brute.—The play on *Capitol* and *capital* is obvious enough.

[353] *Within's* is a contraction of *within this*. The Poet has some contractions even

OPHELIA. Nay, 'tis twice two months, my lord.

HAMLET. So long? Nay then, let the devil wear black, for I'll have a suit of sabell.[354] O heavens! die two months ago, and not forgotten yet? Then there's hope a great man's memory may outlive his life half a year: but, by'r lady, he must build churches, then; or else shall he suffer not thinking on, with the hobby-horse, whose epitaph is 'For, O, for, O, the hobby-horse is forgot.'[355]

[*Hautboys play. The Dumb Show enters.*]

[*Enter a* KING *and a* QUEEN *very lovingly; the* QUEEN *embracing him, and he her. She kneels, and makes show of protestation unto him. He takes her up, and declines his head upon her neck: lays him down upon a bank of flowers: she, seeing him asleep, leaves him. Anon comes in a fellow, takes off his crown, kisses it, and pours poison in the* KING'*s ears, and exit. The* QUEEN *returns; finds the* KING *dead, and makes passionate action. The Poisoner, with some two or three Mutes, comes in again, seeming to lament with her. The dead body is carried away. The Poisoner woos the* QUEEN *with gifts: she seems loath and unwilling awhile, but in the end accepts his love.*[356]]

[*Exeunt.*]

OPHELIA. What means this, my lord?

HAMLET. Marry, this is miching mallecho;[357] it means mischief.

OPHELIA. Belike this show imports the argument of the play.

---

harsher than this.

[354] *Sabell* is a *flame-colour. A* writer in *The Critic* for 1854, page 373, remarks that "*sabell* or *sabelle* is properly a fawn-colour a good deal heightened with red, and that the term came from the French *couleur d'isabelle.*" According to the *Dictionary of the French Academy, isabelle* is a colour "between white and *yellow*, but with the yellow predominating." It is therefore a very showy, flaring colour; as far as possible from mourning.

[355] The *Hobby-horse* was a part of the old Morris-dance, which was used in the May-games. It was the figure of a horse fastened round a man's waist, the man's legs going through the horse's body, and enabling him to walk, but covered by a long footcloth; while false legs appeared where those of the man's should be, astride the horse. The Puritans waged a furious war against the Morris-dance; which caused the Hobby-horse to be left out of it: hence the burden of a song, which passed into a proverb.

[356] As the King does not take fire at this Dumb-show, we may suppose him to be so engaged with some about him, that he does not mark it.

[357] *Miching mallecho* is lurking mischief or evil-doing. To *mich*, for to skulk, to lurk, was an old English verb in common use in Shakespeare's time; and *mallecho* or *malhecho, misdeed,* he borrowed from the Spanish.

[*Enter Prologue.*]

HAMLET. We shall know by this fellow: the players cannot keep counsel; they'll tell all.[358]

OPHELIA. Will he tell us what this show meant?

HAMLET. Ay, or any show that you'll show him: be not you ashamed to show, he'll not shame to tell you what it means.

OPHELIA. You are naught,[359] you are naught: I'll mark the play.

PROLOGUE.   'For us, and for our tragedy,
                          Here stooping to your clemency,
                          We beg your hearing patiently.' [*Exit.*]

HAMLET. Is this a prologue, or the posy[360] of a ring?

OPHELIA. 'Tis brief, my lord.

HAMLET. As woman's love.

[*Enter a* KING *and a* QUEEN.]

PLAYER KING. *Full thirty times hath Phœbus' cart*[361] *gone round*
Neptune's salt wash and Tellus' orbed ground,
And thirty dozen moons with borrow'd sheen
About the world have times twelve thirties been,
Since love our hearts and Hymen did our hands
Unite comutual in most sacred bands.

PLAYER QUEEN. *So many journeys may the sun and moon*
Make us again count o'er ere love be done!
But, woe is me, you are so sick of late,
So far from cheer and from your former state,
That I distrust you.[362] *Yet, though I distrust,*
Discomfort you, my lord, it nothing must:
For women's fear and love holds quantity;[363]
In neither aught, or in extremity.
Now, what my love is, proof hath made you know;
And as my love is sized, my fear is so:

---

[358] Hamlet is running a high strain of jocularity with Ophelia, in order to hide his purpose. The wit here turns upon the fact, that an actor's business is speaking; blurting out before the world what would else be unknown; as dramatic personages are always supposed to be speaking, as *without an audience,* what an audience is nevertheless listening to. Hence they are ever blabbing to the public the things they confide to each other.

[359] That is, *naughty, bad* . not *nothing* or *nought.*

[360] The *posy* is the *motto,* or words inscribed, and of course very brief.

[361] *Cart, car,* and *chariot* were used indiscriminately.—"The style," says Coleridge, "of the interlude here is distinguished from the real dialogue by rhyme, as in the first interview with the players by epic verse."

[362] "Distrust *your health*"; "am solicitous about you."

[363] "Hold quantity" is *have equal strength.*

Where love is great, the littlest doubts are fear;
Where little fears grow great, great love grows there.
PLAYER KING. *Faith, I must leave thee, love, and shortly too;*
My operant[364] powers their functions leave to do:
And thou shalt live in this fair world behind,
Honour'd, beloved; and haply one as kind
For husband shalt thou—
PLAYER QUEEN. *O, confound the rest!*
Such love must needs be treason in my breast:
In second husband let me be accurst!
None wed the second but who kill'd the first.
HAMLET. [*Aside.*] Wormwood, wormwood.
PLAYER QUEEN. *The instances[365] that second marriage move*
Are base respects of thrift, but none of love:
A second time I kill my husband dead,
When second husband kisses me in bed.
PLAYER KING. *I do believe you think what now you speak;*
But what we do determine oft we break.
Purpose is but the slave to memory,
Of violent birth, but poor validity;
Which now, like fruit unripe, sticks on the tree;
But fall, unshaken, when they mellow be.
Most necessary[366] 'tis that we forget
To pay ourselves what to ourselves is debt:
What to ourselves in passion we propose,
The passion ending, doth the purpose lose.
The violence of either grief or joy
Their own enactures[367] with themselves destroy:
Where joy most revels, grief doth most lament;
Grief joys, joy grieves, on slender accident.
This world is not for aye, nor 'tis not strange
That even our loves should with our fortunes change;
For 'tis a question left us yet to prove,
Whether love lead fortune, or else fortune love.
The great man down, you mark his favourite flies;
The poor advanced makes friends of enemies.
And hitherto doth love on fortune tend;
For who not needs shall never lack a friend,
And who in want a hollow friend doth try,

---

[364] *Operant* for *active* or *operative*. So in *Timon of Athens*, iv. 3: "Sauce his palate with thy most *operant* poison."

[365] *Instances* for *inducements*. In the next line, *respects* is *considerations* or *motives*, as usual in Shakespeare.

[366] Necessary here means *natural* or *unavoidable*. Repeatedly so.

[367] *Enactures* for *determinations*; what they *enact*.

> *Directly seasons him his enemy.*
> *But, orderly to end where I begun,*
> *Our wills and fates do so contrary run*
> *That our devices still are overthrown;*
> *Our thoughts are ours, their ends none of our own:*[368]
> *So think thou wilt no second husband wed;*
> *But die thy thoughts when thy first lord is dead.*

PLAYER QUEEN. *Nor earth to me give food, nor heaven light!*
> *Sport and repose lock from me day and night!*
> *To desperation turn my trust and hope!*
> *An anchor's cheer*[369] *in prison be my scope!*
> *Each opposite that blanks the face of joy*[370]
> *Meet what I would have well and it destroy!*
> *Both here and hence pursue me lasting strife,*
> *If, once a widow, ever I be wife!*

HAMLET. If she should break it now!

PLAYER KING. *'Tis deeply sworn. Sweet, leave me here awhile;*
> *My spirits grow dull, and fain I would beguile*
> *The tedious day with sleep.* [*Sleeps.*]

PLAYER QUEEN. *Sleep rock thy brain,*
> *And never come mischance between us twain!* [*Exit.*]

HAMLET. Madam, how like you this play?

QUEEN. The lady protests too much, methinks.

HAMLET. O, but she'll keep her word.

KING. Have you heard the argument? Is there no offence in 't?

HAMLET. No, no, they do but jest, poison in jest; no offence i' the world.

KING. What do you call the play?

HAMLET. The Mouse-trap. Marry, how? Tropically.[371] This play is the image of a murder done in Vienna: Gonzago is the duke's name; his wife, Baptista: you shall see anon; 'tis a knavish piece of work: but what o' that? your majesty and we that have free souls, it touches us not: let the galled jade wince, our withers are unwrung.[372]

[*Enter* LUCIANUS.]

This is one Lucianus, nephew to the king.

---

[368] That is, we can *control* our thoughts, but not their *results.*

[369] A *hermit's fare,* or *diet. Anchor* for *anchoret,* an old word for *hermit.*

[370] To *blank* the face is to make it *white;* to take the blood out of it. The proper colour of joy is *ruddy.*

[371] *Tropically* is *figuratively,* or in the way of trope.

[372] The allusion is to a horse wincing as the saddle galls his withers.

OPHELIA. You are as good as a chorus,[373] my lord.

HAMLET. I could interpret between you and your love,[374] if I could see the puppets dallying.

OPHELIA. You are keen, my lord, you are keen.

HAMLET. It would cost you a groaning to take off my edge.

OPHELIA. Still better, and worse.

HAMLET. So you must take your husbands. Begin, murderer; pox, leave thy damnable faces, and begin. Come: 'the croaking raven doth bellow for revenge.'[375]

LUCIANUS. *Thoughts black, hands apt, drugs fit, and time agreeing;*
Confederate season, else no creature seeing;[376]
Thou mixture rank, of midnight weeds collected,
With Hecate's ban thrice blasted,[377] *thrice infected,*
Thy natural magic and dire property,
On wholesome life usurp immediately.

[*Pours the poison into the sleeper's ears.*]

HAMLET. He poisons him i' the garden for's estate. His name's Gonzago: the story is extant, and writ in choice Italian: you shall see anon how the murderer gets the love of Gonzago's wife.

OPHELIA. The king rises.

HAMLET. What, frighted with false fire!

QUEEN. How fares my lord?

POLONIUS. Give o'er the play.

KING. Give me some light: away!

ALL. Lights, lights, lights!

[*Exeunt all but* HAMLET *and* HORATIO.]

HAMLET.   Why, let the stricken deer go weep,
                  The hart ungalled play;[378]
            For some must watch, while some must sleep:

---

[373] The use to which Shakespeare put the *chorus* may be seen in *King Henry V.* Every motion or puppet-show was accompanied by an *interpreter* or showman.

[374] *Love* for *lover*; a very common usage.

[375] "The croaking raven," &c, is probably a quotation from some play then well known. The raven's croak was thought to be ill-boding.

[376] No creature but time looking on, and that a confederate in the act, or conspiring with the murderer.

[377] Poisonous weeds were supposed to be more poisonous if gathered in the night. *Hecate* was the name given to the Queen of the witches; and her *banning* or cursing brought the poison to the highest intensity.

[378] It is said that a deer, when badly wounded, retires from the herd, and goes apart, to weep and die. Of course, *hart* is the same as *deer*, and *un*galled the opposite of *strucken*.

So runs the world away.

Would not this, sir, and a forest of feathers[379]—if the rest of my fortunes turn Turk with me—with two Provincial roses on my razed shoes,[380] get me a fellowship in a cry of players, sir?[381]

HORATIO. Half a share.[382]

HAMLET. A whole one, I.
　　　　For thou dost know, O Damon dear,
　　　　　　This realm dismantled was
　　　　Of Jove himself;[383] and now reigns here
　　　　　A very, very—pajock.[384]

HORATIO. You might have rhymed.[385]

HAMLET. O good Horatio, I'll take the ghost's word for a thousand pound. Didst perceive?

HORATIO. Very well, my lord.

---

[379] Alluding, probably, to a custom which the London players had in Shakespeare's time, of flaunting it in gaudy apparel, and with *plumes* in their caps, the more the better. So in Chapman's *Monsieur D'Olive*, 1606, iii. 1: "Three of these goldfinches I have entertained for my followers: I am ashamed to train 'em abroad; they say I carry a whole *forest of feathers* with me." It was matter of complaint with some, that many "proud players jet in their silks."—To *turn Turk* with any one was to *desert* or *betray* him, or turn traitor to him. A common phrase of the time.

[380] *Provincial* roses took their name from *Provins*, in Lower Brie, and not from *Provence*. *Razed* shoes are most probably *embroidered* shoes. To *race*, or *raze*, was to *stripe*.

[381] "A *fellowship* in a *cry* of players" is a *partnership* in a *company* of players. The Poet repeatedly uses *cry* thus for *set*, *pack*, or *troop*. The word was borrowed from the chase, as hounds were selected for a pack according to their barking tones.

[382] The players were paid not by salaries, but by *shares* or portions of the profit, according to merit. Perhaps, however, the allusion is rather to the custom, then in vogue, of making the theatrical property a joint-stock affair. Thus Shakespeare himself was a stockholder in the Globe theatre, and so had not only his portion of the profits as one of the players, but also an income from the money invested, or from the shares he held in the stock.

[383] The meaning is, that Denmark was robbed of a king who had the majesty of Jove.—Hamlet calls Horatio Damon, in allusion to the famous friendship of Damon and Pythias.

[384] *Pajock* is probably an old form of *peacock*. Dyce says he has "often heard the lower classes in the north of Scotland call the peacock *peajock*." Editors have been greatly in the dark as to the reason of the word's being used here. But a writer in *The Edinburgh Review*, October, 1872, shows that in the popular belief of Shakespeare's time the peacock had a very bad character, "being, in fact, the accredited representative of inordinate pride and envy, as well as of unnatural cruelty and lust." And he quotes from what was then the most popular manual of natural history: "The peacocke, as one sayth, hath the voice of a feend, the head of a serpent, and the pace of a theefe." The writer adds that "in the whole fauna of the time Hamlet could not have selected the name of bird or beast that expressed with greater emphasis the hateful union of corrupted passion and evil life that now usurped the throne of Denmark."

[385] *Ass* was often used as a rhyme to *was*.

HAMLET. Upon the talk of the poisoning?

HORATIO. I did very well note him.

HAMLET. Ah, ha! Come, some music! come, the recorders![386]
    For if the king like not the comedy,
    Why then, belike, he likes it not, perdy.[387]
    Come, some music!

[*Re-enter* ROSENCRANTZ *and* GUILDENSTERN.]

GUILDENSTERN. Good my lord, vouchsafe me a word with you.

HAMLET. Sir, a whole history.

GUILDENSTERN. The king, sir,—

HAMLET. Ay, sir, what of him?

GUILDENSTERN. Is in his retirement marvellous distempered.

HAMLET. With drink, sir?

GUILDENSTERN. No, my lord, rather with choler.

HAMLET. Your wisdom should show itself more richer to signify this
    to his doctor; for, for me to put him to his purgation would perhaps
    plunge him into far more choler.

GUILDENSTERN. Good my lord, put your discourse into some frame
    and start not so wildly from my affair.

HAMLET. I am tame, sir: pronounce.

GUILDENSTERN. The queen, your mother, in most great affliction of
    spirit, hath sent me to you.

HAMLET. You are welcome.

GUILDENSTERN. Nay, good my lord, this courtesy is not of the right
    breed. If it shall please you to make me a wholesome answer, I will
    do your mother's commandment: if not, your pardon and my return
    shall be the end of my business.

HAMLET. Sir, I cannot.

GUILDENSTERN. What, my lord?

HAMLET. Make you a wholesome answer; my wit's diseased: but, sir,
    such answer as I can make, you shall command; or, rather, as you
    say, my mother: therefore no more, but to the matter: my mother,
    you say,—

ROSENCRANTZ. Then thus she says; your behavior hath struck her
    into amazement and admiration.[388]

HAMLET. O wonderful son, that can so astonish a mother! But is there
    no sequel at the heels of this mother's admiration? Impart.

ROSENCRANTZ. She desires to speak with you in her closet, ere you
    go to bed.

---

[386] The recorder was a soft-toned instrument, something like the flute.

[387] *Perdy* is an old corruption of the French *par Dieu.*

[388] *Admiration*, again, in its proper Latin sense of *wonder.*

HAMLET. We shall obey, were she ten times our mother. Have you any further trade with us?

ROSENCRANTZ. My lord, you once did love me.

HAMLET. So I do still, by these pickers and stealers.[389]

ROSENCRANTZ. Good my lord, what is your cause of distemper? You do, surely, bar the door upon your own liberty, if you deny your griefs to your friend.

HAMLET. Sir, I lack advancement.

ROSENCRANTZ. How can that be, when you have the voice of the king himself for your succession in Denmark?

HAMLET. Ay, but sir, 'While the grass grows,'—the proverb is something musty.[390]

[*Re-enter Players, with recorders.*]

O, the recorders! let me see one. To withdraw with you: [*Takes* GUILDENSTERN *aside.*] Why do you go about to recover the wind of me, as if you would drive me into a toil?[391]

GUILDENSTERN. O, my lord, if my duty be too bold, my love is too unmannerly.[392]

HAMLET. I do not well understand that. Will you play upon this pipe?

GUILDENSTERN. My lord, I cannot.

HAMLET. I pray you.

GUILDENSTERN. Believe me, I cannot.

HAMLET. I do beseech you.

GUILDENSTERN. I know no touch of it, my lord.

HAMLET. It is as easy as lying: govern these ventages with your fingers and thumb, give it breath with your mouth, and it will discourse most eloquent music. Look you, these are the stops.[393]

GUILDENSTERN. But these cannot I command to any utterance of harmony; I have not the skill.

HAMLET. Why, look you now, how unworthy a thing you make of me! You would play upon me; you would seem to know my stops; you would pluck out the heart of my mystery; you would sound me from my lowest note to the top of my compass: and there is much

---

[389] This is explained by a clause in the Church Catechism: "To keep my *hands* from *picking* and *stealing.*"—In "So I do still," *so* is emphatic, and strongly ironical.

[390] "The musty proverb" is, "Whylst grass doth growe, oft sterves the seely steede."

[391] "To *recover* the *wind* of me "is a term borrowed from hunting, and means to take advantage of the animal pursued, by getting to the windward of it, that it may not scent its pursuers.—*Toil* is *snare* or *trap.*

[392] Hamlet may well say, "I do not well understand that." The meaning, however, seems to be, "If I am using an unmannerly boldness with you, it is my love that makes me do so."

[393] The *ventages* are the holes of the pipe. *Stops* signifies the mode of stopping the ventages so as to make the notes.

music, excellent voice, in this little organ; yet cannot you make it speak. 'Sblood, do you think I am easier to be played on than a pipe? Call me what instrument you will, though you can fret me,[394] yet you cannot play upon me.

[*Re-enter* POLONIUS.]

God bless you, sir!
POLONIUS. My lord, the queen would speak with you, and presently.
HAMLET. Do you see yonder cloud that's almost in shape of a camel?
POLONIUS. By the mass, and 'tis like a camel, indeed.
HAMLET. Methinks it is like a weasel.
POLONIUS. It is backed like a weasel.
HAMLET. Or like a whale?
POLONIUS. Very like a whale.
HAMLET. Then I will come to my mother by and by. [*Aside.*] They
    fool me to the top of my bent.[395]—I will come by and by.
POLONIUS. I will say so. [*Exit* POLONIUS.]
HAMLET. By and by is easily said.—Leave me, friends.—

[*Exeunt all but* HAMLET.]

'Tis now the very witching time of night,
When churchyards yawn[396] and hell itself breathes out
Contagion to this world: now could I drink hot blood,
And do such bitter business as the day
Would quake to look on. Soft! now to my mother.—
O heart, lose not thy nature; let not ever
The soul of Nero[397] enter this firm bosom:
Let me be cruel, not unnatural:
I will speak daggers to her, but use none;
My tongue and soul in this be hypocrites;
How in my words soever she be shent,[398]

---

[394] Hamlet keeps up the allusion to a musical instrument. The *frets* of a lute or guitar are the ridges crossing the finger-board, upon which the strings are pressed or *stopped.* A quibble is intended on *fret.*

[395] They *humour* me to the *full height* of my inclination. Polonius has been using the method, common in the treatment of crazy people, of assenting to all that Hamlet says. This is what Hamlet refers to.

[396] Churchyards *yawn* to let forth the ghosts, who did all their walking in the night. And the crimes which darkness so often covers might well be spoken of as caused by the nocturnal contagion of Hell.

[397] Nero is aptly referred to here, as he was the murderer of his mother, Agrippina. It may be worth noting that the name of the King in this play is *Claudius*; and that, after the death of Domitius her husband, Agrippina married with her uncle the Emperor Claudius.

[398] To *shend* is to *injure*, whether by reproof, blows, or otherwise. Shakespeare generally uses *shent* for *reproved*, threatened with angry words. "To give his words

To give them seals never, my soul, consent! [*Exit.*]

SCENE III.

A Room in the Castle.

[*Enter the* KING, ROSENCRANTZ, *and* GUILDENSTERN.]

KING. I like him not, nor stands it safe with us
    To let his madness range. Therefore prepare you;
    I your commission will forthwith dispatch,
    And he to England shall along with you:
    The terms of our estate may not endure
    Hazard so dangerous as doth hourly grow
    Out of his lunacies.
GUILDENSTERN. We will ourselves provide:
    Most holy and religious fear it is
    To keep those many many bodies safe
    That live and feed upon your majesty.
ROSENCRANTZ. The single and peculiar life is bound,
    With all the strength and armour of the mind,
    To keep itself from noyance; but much more
    That spirit upon whose weal depend and rest
    The lives of many. The cease of majesty
    Dies not alone;[399] but, like a gulf, doth draw
    What's near it with it: it is a massy wheel,
    Fix'd on the summit of the highest mount,
    To whose huge spokes ten thousand lesser things
    Are mortised and adjoin'd; which, when it falls,
    Each small annexment, petty consequence,
    Attends the boisterous ruin. Never alone
    Did the king sigh, but with a general groan.
KING. Arm you, I pray you, to this speedy voyage;
    For we will fetters put upon this fear,
    Which now goes too free-footed.
ROSENCRANTZ. We will haste us.

[*Exeunt* ROSENCRANTZ *and* GUILDENSTERN.]

[*Enter* POLONIUS.]

---

seals" is therefore to carry his punishment beyond *reproof.* The allusion is to the sealing of a deed to render it effective.
    [399] Tautological in word, but not in sense. The cease (*decease*) of majesty *comes* not alone.

POLONIUS. My lord, he's going to his mother's closet:
    Behind the arras I'll convey myself,
    To hear the process; and warrant she'll tax him home:[400]
    And, as you said, and wisely was it said,
    'Tis meet that some more audience than a mother,
    Since nature makes them partial, should o'erhear
    The speech, of vantage.[401] Fare you well, my liege:
    I'll call upon you ere you go to bed,
    And tell you what I know.
KING. Thanks, dear my lord.—[*Exit* POLONIUS.]
    O, my offence is rank it smells to heaven;
    It hath the primal eldest curse upon't—
    A brother's murder. Pray can I not,
    Though inclination be as sharp as will:
    My stronger guilt defeats my strong intent;[402]
    And, like a man to double business bound,
    I stand in pause where I shall first begin,
    And both[403] neglect. What if this cursed hand
    Were thicker than itself with brother's blood,
    Is there not rain enough in the sweet heavens
    To wash it white as snow? Whereto serves mercy
    But to confront the visage of offence?
    And what's in prayer but this two-fold force,
    To be forestalled ere we come to fall,
    Or pardon'd being down?[404] Then I'll look up;
    My fault is past. But, O, what form of prayer
    Can serve my turn? 'Forgive me my foul murder'?
    That cannot be; since I am still possess'd
    Of those effects for which I did the murder—
    My crown, mine own ambition and my queen.
    May one be pardon'd and retain the offence?
    In the corrupted currents of this world
    Offence's gilded hand may shove by justice,
    And oft 'tis seen the wicked prize itself
    Buys out the law: but 'tis not so above;

---

[400] *Home* as a general intensive, meaning *thoroughly, to the utmost.*

[401] Speech having an advantage in that nature makes the speakers partial to each other. This favours the conclusion that the Queen was not privy and consenting to the murder of Hamlet's father. Both the King and Polonius have some distrust of her.

[402] "Though I were not only willing but strongly inclined to pray, my guilt would prevent me." The distinction here implied is philosophically just. The inclination is the craving or the impulse to assuage his pangs of remorse; the will is the determination of the reason or judgment in a question of duty and right.

[403] *Both* refers to the *two matters* of business implied in *double.*

[404] That is, either to be *prevented from falling,* or to be pardoned *after we have fallen.* Alluding to a part of the Lord's Prayer.

There is no shuffling, there the action lies
In his true nature; and we ourselves compell'd,
Even to the teeth and forehead of our faults,
To give in evidence. What then? what rests?[405]
Try what repentance can: what can it not?
Yet what can it when one can not repent?
O wretched state! O bosom black as death!
O limed soul,[406] that, struggling to be free,
Art more engaged! Help, angels! Make assay!
Bow, stubborn knees; and, heart with strings of steel,
Be soft as sinews of the newborn babe!
All may be well.[407] [*Retires and kneels.*]

[*Enter* HAMLET.]

HAMLET. Now might I do it pat, now he is praying;
And now I'll do't. And so he goes to heaven;
And so am I revenged. That would be scann'd:[408]
A villain kills my father; and for that,
I, his sole son, do this same villain send
To Heaven.
O, this is hire and salary, not revenge.
He took my father grossly, full of bread;
With all his crimes[409] broad blown, as flush as May;
And how his audit stands who knows save heaven?
But in our circumstance and course of thought,[410]
'Tis heavy with him: and am I then revenged,
To take him in the purging of his soul,
When he is fit and season'd for his passage?
No!
Up, sword; and know thou a more horrid hent.[411]
When he is drunk asleep, or in his rage,

---

[405] "What *remains* to be done?" or, "What *else* can I do?"

[406] Alluding to an old mode of catching birds, by spreading upon the twigs, where they are likely to light, a sticky substance called *bird-lime.*

[407] The final "All may be well" is remarkable;—the degree of merit attributed by the self-flattering soul to its own struggles, though baffled, and to the indefinite half promise, half command, to persevere in religious duties.—COLERIDGE.

[408] That *should* be *scrutinized.*

[409] *Crimes* in the more general sense of *sins.* So twice before in this play: "The foul *crimes* done in my days of nature"; and, "Having ever seen in the predominate *crimes* the youth you breathe of."

[410] "Circumstance and course of thought" seems to mean the particular data or circumstantial detail of things from which our thought shapes its course and draws its conclusions.

[411] *Hent,* both noun and verb, was used in the sense of *seizure, grasp,* or *hold.* Here it has the kindred sense of *purpose.*

Or in the incestuous pleasure of his bed;
At gaming, swearing, or about some act
That has no relish of salvation in't—
Then trip him, that his heels may kick at heaven,
And that his soul may be as damn'd and black
As hell, whereto it goes.[412] My mother stays:
This physic but prolongs thy sickly days.[413] [*Exit.*]

[*The* KING *rises and advances.*]

KING. [*Rising.*] My words fly up, my thoughts remain below:
    Words without thoughts never to heaven go. [*Exit.*]

SCENE IV.

The QUEEN'*s Chamber.*

[*Enter the* QUEEN *and* POLONIUS.]

POLONIUS. 'A will come straight. Look you lay home to him:
    Tell him his pranks have been too broad to bear with,
    And that your grace hath screen'd and stood between
    Much heat and him. I'll sconce me even here.
    Pray you, be round with him.
HAMLET. [*Within.*] Mother, mother, mother!
QUEEN. I'll warrant you,
    Fear me not: withdraw, I hear him coming.

[POLONIUS *hides behind the arras.*]

[*Enter* HAMLET.]

HAMLET. Now, mother, what's the matter?
QUEEN. Hamlet, thou hast thy father much offended.
HAMLET. Mother, you have my father much offended.

---

[412] Hamlet here flies off to a sort of *ideal* revenge, in order to quiet his filial feelings without crossing his reason. Yet it is a very mark-worthy fact, that the King is taken at last in the perpetration of crimes far worse than any that Hamlet here anticipates. But that, to be sure, is the Poet's ordering of the matter, and perhaps should be regarded as expressing *his* sense of justice in this case; though Hamlet may well be supposed to have a presentiment, that a man so bad, and so secure in his badness, will not rest where he is; but will proceed to some further exploiting in crime, in the midst of which judgment will at last overtake him.

[413] *This physic* refers to the reasons Hamlet has been giving for not striking now; a medicine that prolongs the King's sickness, but does not heal it; that is, the purpose is delayed, not abandoned.

QUEEN. Come, come, you answer with an idle tongue.

HAMLET. Go, go, you question with a wicked tongue.

QUEEN. Why, how now, Hamlet!

HAMLET. What's the matter now?

QUEEN. Have you forgot me?

HAMLET. No, by the rood,[414] not so:
    You are the queen, your husband's brother's wife;
    And—would it were not so!—you are my mother.

QUEEN. Nay, then, I'll set those to you that can speak.

HAMLET. Come, come, and sit you down; you shall not budge;
    You go not till I set you up a glass
    Where you may see the inmost part of you.

QUEEN. What wilt thou do? thou wilt not murder me?
    Help, help, ho!

POLONIUS. [*Behind.*] What, ho! help, help, help!

HAMLET. [*Drawing.*] How now! a rat? Dead, for a ducat, dead!
    [*Makes a pass through the arras.*]

POLONIUS. [*Behind.*] O, I am slain! [*Falls and dies.*]

QUEEN. O me, what hast thou done?

HAMLET. Nay, I know not:
    Is it the king?

QUEEN. O, what a rash and bloody deed is this!

HAMLET. A bloody deed!—almost as bad, good mother,
    As kill a king, and marry with his brother.

QUEEN. As kill a king!

HAMLET. Ay, lady, 'twas my word.—

[*Lifts up the arras, and sees* POLONIUS.]

Thou wretched, rash, intruding fool, farewell!
    I took thee for thy better: take thy fortune;
    Thou find'st to be too busy is some danger.
    Leave wringing of your hands: peace! sit you down,
    And let me wring your heart; for so I shall,
    If it be made of penetrable stuff,
    If damned custom have not braz'd it so
    That it is proof and bulwark against sense.

QUEEN. What have I done, that thou dar'st wag thy tongue
    In noise so rude against me?

HAMLET. Such an act
    That blurs the grace and blush of modesty,
    Calls virtue hypocrite,[415] takes off the rose

---

[414] *Rood* is an old word for *cross*; often used for an oath, as here.

[415] A thing is often said to do that which it any way causes to be done.

From the fair forehead of an innocent love
And sets a blister there, makes marriage-vows
As false as dicers' oaths: O, such a deed
As from the body of contraction plucks
The very soul,[416] and sweet religion makes
A rhapsody of words: heaven's face doth glow:
Yea, this solidity and compound mass,[417]
With heated visage, as against the doom,
Is thought-sick at the act.

QUEEN. Ay me, what act,
That roars so loud, and thunders in the index?[418]

HAMLET. Look here, upon this picture, and on this,
The counterfeit presentment[419] of two brothers.
See, what a grace was seated on this brow;
Hyperion's curls; the front of Jove himself;[420]
An eye like Mars, to threaten and command;
A station[421] like the herald Mercury
New-lighted on a heaven-kissing hill—
A combination and a form indeed,
Where every god did seem to set his seal,
To give the world assurance of a man:
This was your husband. Look you now, what follows:
Here is your husband; like a mildew'd ear,
Blasting his wholesome brother.[422] Have you eyes?
Could you on this fair mountain leave to feed,
And batten[423] on this moor? Ha! have you eyes?

---

[416] *Contraction* here means the *marriage contract*; of which Hamlet holds religion to be the life and soul, insomuch that without this it is but as a lifeless body, and must soon become a nuisance.

[417] That is the Earth. Hamlet in his high-wrought stress of passion, kindling as he goes on, makes the fine climax, that not only the heavenly powers burn with indignation, but even the gross beings of this world are smitten with grief and horror, as if the day of judgment were at hand.

[418] The *index*, or table of contents, was formerly placed at the beginning of books. In *Othello*, ii. 1, we have, "an *index* and obscure *prologue* to the history of lust and foul thoughts."

[419] *Counterfeit presentment*, or *counterfeit* simply, was used for *likeness*. It is to be supposed that Hamlet wears a miniature of his father, while his mother wears one of the present King.

[420] The statues of Jupiter represented him as the most intellectual of all the gods, as Apollo was the most beautiful; while in Mercury we have the ideal of swiftness and dispatch.

[421] *Station* does not here mean the spot where any one is placed, but the *act of standing*, the *attitude*. So in *Antony and Cleopatra*, iii. 3: "Her motion and her *station* are as one."

[422] The allusion is to the blasted ears of corn that destroyed the full and good ears, in Pharaoh's dream; *Genesis*, xli. 5-7.

[423] To *batten* is to *feed rankly* or *grossly*; it is usually applied to the fattening of

You cannot call it love; for at your age
The hey-day in the blood is tame, it's humble,
And waits upon the judgment: and what judgment
Would step from this to this? Sense, sure, you have,
Else could you not have motion; but sure, that sense
Is apoplex'd;[424] for madness would not err,
Nor sense to ecstasy was ne'er so thrall'd
But it reserved some quantity of choice,[425]
To serve in such a difference. What devil was't
That thus hath cozen'd you at hoodman-blind?[426]
Eyes without feeling, feeling without sight,
Ears without hands or eyes, smelling sans all,
Or but a sickly part of one true sense
Could not so mope.[427]
O shame! where is thy blush? Rebellious hell,
If thou canst mutine[428] in a matron's bones,
To flaming youth let virtue be as wax,
And melt in her own fire:[429] proclaim no shame

animals.
[424] There is some confusion here, owing to the different meanings with which *sense* is used. The first *sense* is *sensation*; the second refers to the mind. In our usage, the word *brain* would best combine those meanings, thus: "You have *brains*, else you could not have motion; but, surely, your *brain* is palsied." The idea seems to be, that her mind is not merely untuned, as in madness, but absolutely quenched or gone.—In "madness would not err," the meaning is, "madness would not *so* err."
[425] Sense was never so *dominated* by the delusions of *insanity*, but that it still retained *some power* of choice. We have before had *quantity* in much the same sense.
[426] *Hoodman-blind* is the old game of *blindman's-buff*.
[427] To *mope* is to be *dull and stupid*.
[428] *Mutine* for *mutiny*. This is the old form of the verb. Shakespeare calls *mutineers mutines* in a subsequent scene.
[429] Another instance like that of note 424; there being a confusion of the fire which is indeed the life of virtue with that which consumes her. For *her own* clearly refers to *virtue*; else the words *in her own fire* are much worse than useless, as having no effect but to clog or cloud the meaning; and if, as some do, we take them as referring to *youth*, we then have the poor platitude, "to the fire of youth let virtue be as wax, and melt in the fire of youth." Now *virtue's own fire* can hardly mean the fire that consumes virtue. But there is, in the moral sense, a fire that cleanses and preserves, and there is also a fire that corrupts and destroys; and the text involves a verbal identification of the two. So that we have here a very pregnant note of the Poet's, or of Hamlet's, ethical creed. For virtue is not a cold, calculating thing: she is a *passion*, or she is truly nothing: she must have her altar, and her vestal fire ever burning there, else she will die: as the author of *Ecce Homo* observes, "No heart is pure that is not passionate; no virtue is safe that is not enthusiastic." And the generous, or, if you please, the romantic, fire of young enthusiasm is truly the vestal flame in and by which virtue lives. But the case is indeed wellnigh desperate, when impurity usurps the passion that rightly belongs to purity, and when virtue perishes by the fire of her own altar. And the very pith of Hamlet's censure is, that the sacred fire of noble passion, which burns so savingly in youth,—a fire kindled and fed with the idea of moral beauty;—that this fire has, in his mother's matron age, inverted itself into the unholy and destructive fire of lust.—Several persons have snapped me

When the compulsive ardour gives the charge,
Since frost itself as actively doth burn
And reason panders will.
QUEEN. O Hamlet, speak no more:
Thou turn'st mine eyes into my very soul;
And there I see such black and grained spots[430]
As will not leave their tinct.
HAMLET. Nay, but to live
In the rank sweat of an enseamed bed,[431]
Stew'd in corruption, honeying and making love
Over the nasty sty,—
QUEEN. O, speak to me no more;
These words, like daggers, enter in mine ears;
No more, sweet Hamlet!
HAMLET. A murderer and a villain;
A slave that is not twentieth part the tithe
Of your precedent lord; a vice of kings;[432]
A cutpurse of the empire and the rule,
That from a shelf the precious diadem stole,[433]
And put it in his pocket!
QUEEN. No more!
HAMLET. A king of shreds and patches—

[*Enter the* GHOST.]

Save me, and hover o'er me with your wings,
You heavenly guards! What would your gracious figure?
QUEEN. Alas, he's mad!
HAMLET. Do you not come your tardy son to chide,
That, lapsed in time and passion,[434] lets go by

---

rather sharply for taking this view of the text; but perhaps there are some things in Shakespeare, *and* in Nature, which they have yet to learn.

[430] That is, spots *ingrained*, or *dyed in the grain.—Tinct* is *colour.*

[431] *Enseamed* is a term borrowed from falconry. *Seam* is fat or grease. Hawks, when kept in mew, became, through inaction and high-feeding, *enseamed,* as it was called, that is, too fat or gross for flight; and, in order to fit them for use, their grossness had to be purged off by a course of scouring diet and medicine. The place where the hawks were kept during this process was apt to get very foul. It is in allusion to this that Hamlet applies the term to the moral pollution of his mother's incestuous marriage, and to the bridal couch itself as being defiled by such a union.

[432] An allusion to the old Vice or jester, a stereotyped character in the Moral-plays, which were going out of use in the Poet's time. The Vice wore a motley or patchwork dress; hence the *shreds and patches* applied in this instance.

[433] This should not be taken as meaning that Claudius is not the lawful King of Denmark. He "stole the diadem," not by an act of direct usurpation, but by murdering the rightful holder of it.

[434] The sense appears to be, having failed *in respect* both of time and of purpose. Or

The important acting of your dread command? O, say!

GHOST. Do not forget: this visitation
Is but to whet thy almost blunted purpose.
But, look, amazement on thy mother sits:
O, step between her and her fighting soul:
Conceit in weakest bodies[435] strongest works:
Speak to her, Hamlet.

HAMLET. How is it with you, lady?

QUEEN. Alas, how is't with you,
That you do bend your eye on vacancy
And with the incorporal air do hold discourse?
Forth at your eyes your spirits wildly peep;
And, as the sleeping soldiers in the alarm,
Your bedded hair, like life in excrements,[436]
Starts up, and stands on end. O gentle son,
Upon the heat and flame of thy distemper
Sprinkle cool patience. Whereon do you look?

HAMLET. On him, on him! Look you, how pale he glares!
His form and cause conjoin'd, preaching to stones,
Would make them capable.[437] Do not look upon me;
Lest with this piteous action you convert
My stern affects:[438] then what I have to do
Will want true colour; tears perchance for blood.

QUEEN. To whom do you speak this?

HAMLET. Do you see nothing there?

QUEEN. Nothing at all; yet all that is I see.

HAMLET. Nor did you nothing hear?

QUEEN. No, nothing but ourselves.

HAMLET. Why, look you there! look, how it steals away!
My father, in his habit as he lived!
Look, where he goes, even now, out at the portal!

[*Exit* GHOST.]

---

it may be, having allowed passion to cool by lapse of time.

[435] *Conceit*, again, for *conception, imagination. Bodies* is here put for *minds*, or *persons*; as *corpora* also is in classical Latin.

[436] That is, like excrements *alive*, or having *life in them. Hair*, nails, feathers, &c, were called *excrements*, as being without life.

[437] Would put sense and understanding into them. The use of *capable* for *susceptible, intelligent*, is not peculiar to Shakespeare.

[438] *Affects* is repeatedly used by Shakespeare for *affections* or *passions*, and may signify any mood or temper of mind looking to action. Hamlet is afraid lest the "piteous action" of the Ghost should make his stern mood of revenge give place to tenderness, so that he will see the ministry enjoined upon him in a false light, and go to shedding tears instead of blood.

QUEEN. This the very coinage of your brain:
This bodiless creation ecstasy
Is very cunning in.[439]
HAMLET. Ecstasy!
My pulse, as yours, doth temperately keep time,
And makes as healthful music: it is not madness
That I have utt'red. Bring me to the test,
And I the matter will re-word; which madness
Would gambol from.[440] Mother, for love of grace,
Lay not that mattering unction to your soul,
That not your trespass, but my madness speaks:
It will but skin and film the ulcerous place,
Whilst rank corruption, mining all within,
Infects unseen. Confess yourself to heaven;
Repent what's past; avoid what is to come;
And do not spread the compost on the weeds,
To make them ranker. Forgive me this my virtue;
For in the fatness of these pursy times
Virtue itself of vice must pardon beg,
Yea, courb[441] and woo for leave to do him good.
QUEEN. O Hamlet, thou hast cleft my heart in twain.
HAMLET. O, throw away the worser part of it,
And live the purer with the other half.
Good night: but go not to mine uncle's bed;
Assume a virtue, if you have it not.
That monster, custom, who all sense doth eat,
Of habits devil, is angel yet in this,[442]
That to the use of actions fair and good
He likewise gives a frock or livery,

---

[439] The Ghost in this scene, as also in the banquet-scene of *Macbeth*, is plainly what we should call a *subjective* ghost; that is, existing only in the heated imagination of the beholder. As the Queen says, insanity is very fertile in such "bodiless creations." It is not so with the apparition in the former scenes, as the Ghost is there seen by other persons. To be sure, it was part of the old belief, that ghosts could, if they chose, make themselves visible only to those with whom they were to deal; but this is just what we mean by *subjective*. The ancients could not take the idea of subjective visions, as we use the term. So that the words here put into the Ghost's mouth are to be regarded as merely the echo of Hamlet's own thoughts.

[440] Mad people, if asked to repeat a thing that they have just said, are apt to go on and say something else without knowing it; thus *gambolling* from the matter which they undertake to re-word. But the test is far from being a sure one; madmen being sometimes as firm and steady in the intellectual faculties as the sanest are.

[441] To *courb* is to *bend, curve*, or *truckle*; from the French *courber*.

[442] The meaning appears to be, that, though custom is a monster that *eats out* all *sensibility* or *consciousness* of evil habits; yet, on the other hand, it is an angel in this respect, that it works in a manner equally favourable to good actions.—In this passage *custom, habit*, and *use* all have about the same meaning; I mean the second *use*,—"For use almost," &c.

That aptly is put on. Refrain to-night,
And that shall lend a kind of easiness
To the next abstinence: the next more easy;
For use almost can change the stamp of nature,
And either the devil, or throw him out[443]
With wondrous potency. Once more, good night:
And when you are desirous to be blest,
I'll blessing beg of you.[444] For this same lord,

[*Pointing to* POLONIUS.]

I do repent: but heaven hath pleased it so,
To punish me with this and this with me,
That I must be their[445] scourge and minister.
I will bestow him, and will answer well
The death I gave him. So, again, good night.
[*Aside.*] I must be cruel, only to be kind:
Thus bad begins and worse remains behind.
One word more, good lady.
QUEEN. What shall I do?
HAMLET. Not this, by no means, that I bid you do:
Let the bloat[446] king tempt you again to bed;
Pinch wanton on your cheek; call you his mouse;[447]
And let him, for a pair of reechy[448] kisses,
Or paddling in your neck with his damn'd fingers,
Make you to ravel all this matter out,
That I essentially am not in madness,
But mad in craft. 'Twere good you let him know;
For who, that's but a queen, fair, sober, wise,
Would from a paddock, from a bat, a gib,[449]
Such dear concernings hide? who would do so?
No, in despite of sense and secrecy,
Unpeg the basket on the house's top.
Let the birds fly, and, like the famous ape,
To try conclusions,[450] in the basket creep,

---

[443] The sense of *out* extends back over *shame*; the meaning being, "And either shame the Devil *out* or *force* him out."

[444] How beautiful this is! Of course Hamlet means that, when he finds his mother on her knees to God, he will be on his knees to her.

[445] The pronoun *their* refers to *Heaven*, which is here used as a collective noun, and put for *heavenly powers*.

[446] *Bloat* for *bloated.* Many preterites were formed so.

[447] *Mouse* was a term of endearment. So in *Anatomy of Melancholy:* "Pleasant names may be invented, bird, *mouse*, lamb, puss, pigeon."

[448] *Reeky* and *reechy* are the same word, and applied to any vaporous exhalation.

[449] A *paddock* is a *toad*; *a gib*, a *cat.*

And break your own neck down.
QUEEN. Be thou assured, if words be made of breath,
    And breath of life, I have no life to breathe
    What thou hast said to me.
HAMLET. I must to England; you know that?
QUEEN. Alack,
    I had forgot. 'tis so concluded on.
HAMLET. There's letters seal'd: and my two schoolfellows,
    Whom I will trust as I will adders fang'd—
    They bear the mandate; they must sweep my way,
    And marshal me to knavery. Let it work;
    For 'tis the sport to have the engineer
    Hoist with his own petar:[451] and't shall go hard
    But I will delve one yard below their mines,
    And blow them at the moon: O, 'tis most sweet,
    When in one line two crafts directly meet.
    This man shall set me packing:[452]
    I'll lug the guts into the neighbour room.
    Mother, good night. Indeed this counsellor
    Is now most still, most secret and most grave,
    Who was in life a foolish prating knave.
    Come, sir, to draw toward an end with you.
    Good night, mother.

[*Exeunt severally*; HAMLET *dragging in* POLONIUS.]

SCENE V.

Another Room in the castle.

[*Enter the* KING, *the* QUEEN, ROSENCRANTZ, *and*
GUILDENSTERN.]

KING. There's matter in these sighs, these profound heaves:
    You must translate: 'tis fit we understand them.
    Where is your son?
QUEEN. Bestow this place on us a little while.

---

    [450] To *try conclusions* is the old phrase for *trying experiments*, or putting a thing to the proof.—The passage alludes, apparently, to some fable or story now quite forgotten. Sir John Suckling, in one of his letters, refers to "the story of the jackanapes and the partridges."
    [451] *Hoist* for *hoisted.—Petar*, now spelt *petard*, is a kind of mortar used for blowing open gates and doors.—"It shall go hard," &c., means, "It must be a hard undertaking indeed, if I do not effect it."
    [452] A phrase from the packing-up of baggage for a march or voyage; hence having the general sense of getting ready, or of being off.

[*Exeunt* ROSENCRANTZ *and* GUILDENSTERN.]

Ah, my good lord, what have I seen to-night!
KING. What, Gertrude? How does Hamlet?
QUEEN. Mad as the sea and wind, when both contend
Which is the mightier: in his lawless fit,
Behind the arras hearing something stir,
Whips out his rapier, cries, 'A rat, a rat!'
And, in this brainish[453] apprehension, kills
The unseen good old man.
KING. O heavy deed!
It had been so with us, had we been there:
His liberty is full of threats to all;
To you yourself, to us, to every one.
Alas, how shall this bloody deed be answer'd?
It will be laid to us, whose providence
Should have kept short, restrain'd and out of haunt,[454]
This mad young man. But so much was our love,
We would not understand what was most fit;
But, like the owner of a foul disease,
To keep it from divulging, let it feed
Even on the pith of Life.[455] Where is he gone?
QUEEN. To draw apart the body he hath kill'd:
O'er whom his very madness, like some ore
Among a mineral of metals base,[456]
Shows itself pure; he weeps for what is done.
KING. O Gertrude, come away!
The sun no sooner shall the mountains touch,
But we will ship him hence: and this vile deed
We must, with all our majesty and skill,
Both countenance and excuse. Ho, Guildenstern!

[*Re-enter* ROSENCRANTZ *and* GUILDENSTERN.]

Friends both, go join you with some further aid:
Hamlet in madness hath Polonius slain,

---

[453] *Brainish* for *brainsick*; that is, *crazy*.

[454] Out of *haunt* means out of *company*; in seclusion.

[455] Certain diseases appear to be attended with an instinct of concealment. I have heard of persons dying of external cancer; yet they had kept so secret about it that their nearest friends had not suspected it.

[456] *Mineral* for *mine*; in accordance with old usage. So Hooker, in *Ecclesiastical Polity*, i. 4, 3, speaks of the fallen Angels as "being dispersed, some on the earth, some in the water, some amongst the *minerals*, dens, and caves, that are under the earth."

And from his mother's closet hath he dragg'd him:
Go seek him out; speak fair, and bring the body
Into the chapel. I pray you, haste in this.

[*Exeunt* ROSENCRANTZ *and* GUILDENSTERN.]

Come, Gertrude, we'll call up our wisest friends;
And let them know, both what we mean to do,
And what's untimely done. So, haply slander—
Whose whisper o'er the world's diameter,
As level as the cannon's to his blank,[457]
Transports his poison's shot—may miss our name,
And hit the woundless air. O, come away!
My soul is full of discord and dismay. [*Exeunt.*]

SCENE VI.

Another Room in the Castle.

[*Enter* HAMLET.]

HAMLET. Safely stowed.
ROSENCRANTZ and GUILDENSTERN. [*Within.*] Hamlet! Lord
    Hamlet!
HAMLET. What noise? who calls on Hamlet? O, here they come.

[*Enter* ROSENCRANTZ *and* GUILDENSTERN.]

ROSENCRANTZ. What have you done, my lord, with the dead body?
HAMLET. Compounded it with dust, whereto 'tis kin.
ROSENCRANTZ. Tell us where 'tis, that we may take it thence
And bear it to the chapel.
HAMLET. Do not believe it.
ROSENCRANTZ. Believe what?
HAMLET. That I can keep your counsel and not mine own. Besides, to
    be demanded of a sponge,[458] what replication should be made by
    the son of a king?
ROSENCRANTZ. Take you me for a sponge, my lord?
HAMLET. Ay, sir, that soaks up the king's countenance, his rewards,
    his authorities. But such officers do the king best service in the

---

[457] As *direct*, or as *sure-aimed*, as the cannon to its *mark*. *Direct* is one of the old
meanings of *level*. The *blank* was the *white* spot at which aim was taken in target-
shooting.
    [458] That is, *on being* demanded *by* a sponge. An instance of the infinitive used
gerundively, or like the Latin *Gerund*.

end: he keeps them, like an ape, in the corner of his jaw; first
mouthed, to be last swallowed:[459] when he needs what you have
gleaned, it is but squeezing you, and, sponge, you shall[460] be dry
again.

ROSENCRANTZ. I understand you not, my lord.

HAMLET. I am glad of it: a knavish speech sleeps in a foolish ear.[461]

ROSENCRANTZ. My lord, you must tell us where the body is, and go
with us to the king.

HAMLET. The body is with the king, but the king is not with the
body.[462] The king is a thing—

GUILDENSTERN. A thing, my lord!

HAMLET. Of nothing: bring me to him. Hide fox, and all after.[463]
[*Exeunt.*]

SCENE VII.

Another Room in the Castle.

[*Enter the* KING, *attended.*]

KING. I have sent to seek him, and to find the body.
How dangerous is it that this man goes loose!
Yet must not we put the strong law on him:
He's loved of the distracted[464] multitude,
Who like not in their judgment, but their eyes;
And where 'tis so, the offender's scourge is weigh'd,
But never the offence.[465] To bear all smooth and even,
This sudden sending him away must seem
Deliberate pause:[466] diseases desperate grown

---

[459] Apes have a pouch on each side of the jaw, in which they stow away the food first taken, and there keep it till they have eaten the rest.

[460] *Shall* for *will*; the two being often used indiscriminately.

[461] Perhaps this is best explained by a passage in *Love's Labours Lost*, v. 2: "A jest's prosperity lies in the ear of him that hears it, never in the tongue of him that makes it."

[462] Hamlet is talking riddles, in order to tease and puzzle his questioners. The meaning of this riddle, to the best of my guessing, is, that the King's body is with the King, but not the King's soul: he's a king without kingliness. Perhaps, however, the passage should be regarded simply as a piece of intentional downright nonsense.

[463] "Hide fox, and all after," was a juvenile sport, most probably what is now called *hide and seek.*

[464] *Distracted* in the sense of *discordant*, or *disagreeing*; sometimes called *many-headed.* Perhaps the sense of *fickle, inconstant*, is also intended.

[465] Who like not what their judgment approves, for they have none, but what pleases their eyes; and in this case the criminal's punishment is considered, but not his crime.

[466] "To keep all things quiet and in order, this sudden act must seem a thing that we *have paused and deliberated upon.*"

By desperate appliance are relieved,
Or not at all.

[*Enter* ROSENCRANTZ.]

How now! what hath befall'n?
ROSENCRANTZ. Where the dead body is bestow'd, my lord,
We cannot get from him.
KING. But where is he?
ROSENCRANTZ. Without, my lord; guarded, to know your pleasure.
KING. Bring him before us.
ROSENCRANTZ. Ho, Guildenstern! bring in my lord.

[*Enter* HAMLET *and* GUILDENSTERN.]

KING. Now, Hamlet, where's Polonius?
HAMLET. At supper.
KING. At supper! where?
HAMLET. Not where he eats, but where he is eaten: a certain
convocation of politic worms are e'en at him.[467] Your worm is
your only emperor for diet: we fat all creatures else to fat us, and
we fat ourselves for maggots: your fat king and your lean beggar is
but variable service, two dishes, but to one table: that's the end.
KING. Alas, alas!
HAMLET. A man may fish with the worm that hath eat of a king, and
cat of the fish that hath fed of that worm.
KING. What dost you mean by this?
HAMLET. Nothing but to show you how a king may go a progress
through the guts of a beggar.[468]
KING. Where is Polonius?
HAMLET. In heaven; send hither to see: if your messenger find him
not there, seek him i' the other place yourself. But indeed, if you
find him not within this month, you shall nose him as you go up
the stairs into the lobby.
KING. [*To some* ATTENDANTS.] Go seek him there.
HAMLET. He will stay till ye come. [*Exeunt Attendants.*]
KING. Hamlet, this deed, for thine especial safety,—
Which we do tender,[469] as we dearly grieve

---

[467] Alluding, probably, to the Diet of Worms, which Protestants regarded as a
convocation of *politicians.* Here, again, I am indebted to Mr. Joseph Crosby, who aptly
prompts me, that there is a further allusion to the character of Polonius; meaning such
worms as might naturally be bred in the carcass of a defunct old political wire-puller.
And he remarks, "Had the old gentleman been conspicuous for his ambition, it would
have been just like Shakespeare to call the worms bred from him *aspiring* worms."

[468] Alluding to the *royal* journeys of state, called *progresses.*

For that which thou hast done,—must send thee hence
With fiery quickness: therefore prepare thyself;
The bark is ready, and the wind at help,
The associates tend,[470] and every thing is bent
For England.
HAMLET. For England!
KING. Ay, Hamlet.
HAMLET. Good.
KING. So is it, if thou knew'st our purposes.
HAMLET. I see a cherub that sees them.[471] But, come; for England!
Farewell, dear mother.
KING. Thy loving father, Hamlet.
HAMLET. My mother: father and mother is man and wife; man and
wife is one flesh; and so, my mother. Come, for England! [*Exit.*]
KING. Follow him at foot; tempt him with speed aboard;
Delay it not; I'll have him hence to-night:
Away! for every thing is seal'd and done
That else leans on the affair: pray you, make haste.

[*Exeunt* ROSENCRANTZ *and* GUILDENSTERN.]

And, England, if my love thou hold'st at aught—
As my great power thereof may give thee sense,
Since yet thy cicatrice looks raw and red
After the Danish sword, and thy free awe
Pays homage to us—thou mayst not coldly set[472]
Our sovereign process; which imports at full,
By letters conjuring[473] to that effect,
The present death of Hamlet. Do it, England;
For like the hectic in my blood he rages,
And thou must cure me: till I know 'tis done,
Howe'er my haps, my joys were ne'er begun.[474] [*Exit.*]

---

[469] To *tender* a thing is to *be careful* of it.

[470] The associates of your voyage *are waiting.*—"The wind *at help*" means the wind *serves,* or is right, to forward you.

[471] Hamlet means that he divines them, or has an inkling of them.

[472] To *set* formerly meant to *estimate.* To *set* much or little by a thing, is to *estimate* it much or little.

[473] In Shakespeare's time the two senses of *conjure* had not acquired each its peculiar way of pronouncing the word. Here *conjuring* has the *first* syllable long, with the sense of *earnestly entreating.*

[474] Of course strict grammar would here require "*will* ne'er *begin*"; the tense being changed for the rhyme.

ACT IV.

SCENE I.

A Plain in Denmark.

[*Enter* FORTINBRAS, *a* CAPTAIN, *and* SOLDIERS, *marching.*]

FORTINBRAS. Go, captain, from me greet the Danish king;
    Tell him that, by his license, Fortinbras
    Craves the conveyance of a promised march
    Over his kingdom. You know the rendezvous.[475]
    If that his majesty would aught with us,
    We shall express our duty in his eye;[476]
    And let him know so.
CAPTAIN. I will do't, my lord.
FORTINBRAS. Go softly on.

[*Exeunt* FORTINBRAS *and* SOLDIERS.]

[*Enter* HAMLET, ROSENCRANTZ, GUILDENSTERN, *and*
    others.]

HAMLET. Good sir, whose powers are these?
CAPTAIN. They are of Norway, sir.
HAMLET. How purposed, sir, I pray you?
CAPTAIN. Against some part of Poland.
HAMLET. Who commands them, sir?
CAPTAIN. The nephews to old Norway, Fortinbras.
HAMLET. Goes it against the main of Poland, sir,
Or for some frontier?
CAPTAIN. Truly to speak, and with no addition,
    We go to gain a little patch of ground
    That hath in it no profit but the name.
    To pay five ducats, five, I would not farm it;[477]

---

[475] The rendezvous here meant is the place where Fortinbras is to wait for the Captain after the latter has done his message to the King.

[476] In the *Regulations for the Establishment of the Queen's Household*, 1627: "All such as doe service *in the queen s eye*" And in *The Establishment of Prince Henry s Household*, 1610: "All such as doe service *in the prince's eye.*" Fortinbras means, "I will wait upon his presence, and pay my respects to him in person."

[477] The meaning is, "I would not pay five ducats for the exclusive privilege of collecting all the revenue it will yield to the State." To *farm* or *farm out* taxes is to sell commissions for collecting them, the buyers to have the privilege of making what they can by the process. Burke uses the word in a like sense in his *Articles of Charge against*

Nor will it yield to Norway or the Pole
A ranker rate, should it be sold in fee.
HAMLET. Why, then the Polack never will defend it.
CAPTAIN. Yes, it is already garrison'd.
HAMLET. Two thousand souls and twenty thousand ducats
    Will not debate the question of this straw:
    This is the imposthume[478] of much wealth and peace,
    That inward breaks, and shows no cause without
    Why the man dies. I humbly thank you, sir.
CAPTAIN. God be wi' you, sir. [*Exit.*]
ROSENCRANTZ. Wilt please you go, my lord?
HAMLET. I'll be with you straight go a little before.—

    [*Exeunt all except* HAMLET.]

How all occasions do inform against me,
And spur my dull revenge! What is a man,
If his chief good and market of his time
Be but to sleep and feed? a beast, no more.
Sure, he that made us with such large discourse,
Looking before and after, gave us not
That capability and god-like reason
To fust in us unused.[479] Now, whether it be
Bestial oblivion, or some craven scruple
Of thinking too precisely on the event,
A thought which, quarter'd, hath but one part wisdom
And ever three parts coward, I do not know
Why yet I live to say 'This thing's to do;'
Sith[480] I have cause and will and strength and means
To do't. Examples gross as earth exhort me:
Witness this army of such mass and charge
Led by a delicate and tender prince,
Whose spirit with divine ambition puff'd[481]
Makes mouths at the invisible event,
Exposing what is mortal and unsure
To all that fortune, death and danger dare,
Even for an egg-shell. Rightly to be great

Hastings: "The *farming* of the defence of a country, being wholly unprecedented and evidently abused, could have no real object but to enrich the contractors at the Company's expense."—*To pay* has the force of *by paying.*

[478] *Imposthume* was in common use for *abscess* in Shakespeare's time. It is a corruption of *apostem.*

[479] To *fust* is to *become mouldy*; an old word now obsolete.

[480] *Sith* is merely an old form of *since*; now quite out of use.

[481] *Puff'd*, here, is *inspired* or *animated.*—To *make mouths* at a thing is to *scorn* it, or *hold it in contempt.*

Is not to stir without great argument,
But greatly to find quarrel in a straw
When honour's at the stake. How stand I then,
That have a father kill'd, a mother stain'd,
Excitements of my reason and my blood,[482]
And let all sleep? while, to my shame, I see
The imminent death of twenty thousand men,
That, for a fantasy and trick of fame,
Go to their graves like beds, fight for a plot
Whereon the numbers cannot try the cause,
Which is not tomb enough and continent[483]
To hide the slain? O, from this time forth,
My thoughts be bloody, or be nothing worth! [*Exit.*]

SCENE II.

Elsinore. A Room in the Castle.

[*Enter the* QUEEN *and* HORATIO.]

QUEEN. I will not speak with her.
GEMTLEMAN. She is importunate, indeed distract:[484]
    Her mood will needs be pitied.
QUEEN. What would she have?
GENTLEMAN. She speaks much of her father; says she hears

---

[482] Provocations which excite both my reason and my passions.

[483] *Continent* means that which contains or encloses. "If there be no fulnesse, then is the *continent* greater than the content."—Bacon's *Advancement of Learning.*—The way Hamlet talks in this and several other places moves me to say somewhat touching his state of mind. He is a man of deep and strong feelings; his sensibilities are quick and keen. But he is also quick and strong in understanding, or in the "large discourse looking before and after." Now his feelings are goading him on to the instant stroke of revenge; nothing else can satisfy them: they are bidding him throw consequences to the winds, and would have him act just as Laertes talks: "To Hell, allegiance! vows, to the blackest devil!" &c. Meanwhile his judgment keeps holding him back, as it certainly should. Hence there springs up a fierce, agonized conflict between these two parts of his inner man; and his feelings become terribly insurgent and clamorous: sometimes they seem to get the upper hand of him; he takes part with them, and goes to pleading their cause most vehemently against his higher self; seeking to ease, or to appease, his heart-agony in overwrought strains of self-reproach, and with hopes of speedy satisfaction. All this is profoundly natural. In action, however, Hamlet stands firm and true to his higher self: here his judgment keeps the upper hand; and though he cannot silence his insurgent feelings, yet, in his strength of will, he can and does overrule them. While the heart is boiling hot within him, and almost ready to burst its case, still his head, though full of power, and though all alive within, remains generally, cool; his passions never, but once, swamping him into an oblivion of the strong *objective* considerations that forbid the stroke.

[484] *Distract* for *distracted*; just as *bloat* and *hoist* before.

There's tricks i' the world; and hems, and beats her heart;
Spurns enviously at straws;[485] speaks things in doubt,
That carry but half sense: her speech is nothing,
Yet the unshaped use of it doth move ·
The hearers to collection;[486] they aim at it,
And botch the words up fit to their own thoughts;
Which, as her winks, and nods, and gestures yield them,
Indeed would make one think there might be thought,
Though nothing sure, yet much unhappily.[487]
HORATIO. 'Twere good she were spoken with; for she may strew
Dangerous conjectures in ill-breeding minds.
QUEEN. Let her come in. [*Exit* HORATIO.]
To my sick soul, as sin's true nature is,
Each toy seems prologue to some great amiss:[488]
So full of artless jealousy is guilt,
It spills itself in fearing to be spilt.

[*Re-enter* HORATIO, *with* OPHELIA.[489]]

OPHELIA. Where is the beauteous majesty of Denmark?
QUEEN. How now, Ophelia!

OPHELIA. [*Sings.*]　'How should I your true love know
　　　　　　　　　From another one?
　　　　　　　　　By his cockle hat and staff,
　　　　　　　　　And his sandal shoon.'[490]

QUEEN. Alas, sweet lady, what imports this song?
OPHELIA. Say you? nay, pray you, mark.

---

[485] *Kicks spitefully* at straws. Such was the common use of *spurn* in the Poet's time. So in *The Merchant*, i. 3: "And foot me as you *spurn* a stranger cur over your threshold." And in *Julius Cæsar*, in. 1: "*I spurn* thee like a cur out of my way."—*Envy* was commonly used for *malice*.

[486] *Collection* is *inference* or *conjecture.—Aim* is *guess*.

[487] *Unhappily* is here used in the sense of *mischievously*.

[488] Shakespeare is not singular in the use of *amiss* as a substantive. "Each *toy*" is each *trifle*.

[489] There is no part of the play more pathetic than this scene; which, I suppose, proceeds from the utter insensibility Ophelia has to her own misfortunes. A great sensibility, or none at all, seems to produce the same effects. In the latter case the audience supply what is wanting, and with the former they sympathize.—SIR JOSHUA REYNOLDS.

[490] These were the badges of pilgrims. The *cockle shell* was an emblem of their intention to go beyond sea. The habit, being held sacred, was often assumed as a disguise in love-adventures.

[*Sings.*]   'He is dead and gone, lady,
                                 He is dead and gone;
                              At his head a grass-green turf,
                                 At his heels a stone.'

QUEEN. Nay, but, Ophelia—
OPHELIA. Pray you, mark.

[*Sings.*] 'White his shroud as the mountain snow'—

[*Enter the* KING.]

QUEEN. Alas, look here, my lord.

OPHELIA. [*Sings.*]—'Larded[491] with sweet flowers
                          Which bewept to the grave did go
                          With true-love showers.'

KING. How do you, pretty lady?
OPHELIA. Well, God dild you![492] They say the owl was a baker's
    daughter.[493] Lord, we know what we are, but know not what we
    may be. God be at your table!
KING. Conceit upon her father.
OPHELIA. Pray you, let's have no words of this; but when they ask
    you what it means, say you this:

[*Sings.*]   To-morrow is Saint Valentine's day,
                 All in the morning betime,
             And I a maid at your window,
                 To be your Valentine.[494]
             Then up he rose, and donn'd his clothes,
                 And dupp'd[495] the chamber-door;

---

[491] *Larded* is *garnished,* or *ornamented.*

[492] God *yield* or *reward* you.

[493] There was a tradition that the Saviour went into a baker's shop and asked for
some bread. The baker put some dough in the oven to bake for Him, and was rebuked by
his daughter for doing so. For this wickedness the daughter was transformed into an owl.

[494] Of course *Valentine* stands for a person here; and it means much the same as
lover or *sweet-heart.* The old use of the name is well shown in Scott's *Fair Maid of
Perth,* where Simon Glover wishes to make a match between his daughter Catharine and
Henry Smith, the hero of the tale. He therefore so arranges matters, that Smith shall be
the first person whom Catharine sees on the morning of St. Valentine's day. This makes
him her Valentine for the year: as such, he may claim a kiss of her on the spot, and also
as often as they meet during the year.

[495] To *dup* is to *do up,* as to *don* is to *do on.*

> Let in the maid, that out a maid
> Never departed more.

KING. Pretty Ophelia!
OPHELIA. Indeed, la, without an oath, I'll make an end on't.

> [*Sings.*] By Gis and by Saint Charity,[496]
>   Alack, and fie for shame!
> Young men will do't, if they come to't;
>   By cock,[497] they are to blame.
> Quoth she, before you tumbled me,
>   You promised me to wed.
> So would I ha' done, by yonder sun,
>   An thou hadst not come to my bed.

KING. How long hath she been thus?
OPHELIA. I hope all will be well. We must be patient: but I cannot choose but weep, to think they should lay him i' the cold ground. My brother shall know of it: and so I thank you for your good counsel. Come, my coach! Good night, ladies; good night, sweet ladies; good night, good night. [*Exit.*]
KING. Follow her close; give her good watch,
  I pray you.—[*Exit* HORATIO.]
  O, this is the poison of deep grief; it springs
  All from her father's death.—O Gertrude, Gertrude,
  When sorrows come, they come not single spies
  But in battalias.[498] First, her father slain:
  Next, your son gone; and he most violent author
  Of his own just remove: the people muddied,
  Thick and unwholesome in their thoughts and whispers,
  For good Polonius' death; and we have done but greenly,
  In hugger-mugger[499] to inter him: poor Ophelia
  Divided from herself and her fair judgment,
  Without the which we are pictures, or mere beasts:
  Last, and as much containing as all these,

---

[496] This use of *Gis* has not been accounted for. Probably it is a corruption, or perhaps a disguise, of the Saviour's name. *Saint* Charity was often used in this way.
[497] The origin and meaning of this oath, also, are wrapped in obscurity. It occurs in several old plays, and Shakespeare has it in at least two other places. Probably it was a corruption, or a disguise, of the sacred name.
[498] Men go out *singly*, or one by one, to act as spies; when they go forth to *fight*, they go in armies.
[499] This phrase was much used, before and in the Poet's time, for any thing done hurriedly and by stealth. Thus Florio explains *clandestinaire*, "to hide or conceal by stealth, or *in hugger-mugger*." And in North's Plutarch Antony urges that Caesar's "body should be honourably buried, and not in *hugger-mugger*."

Her brother is in secret come from France;
Feeds on his wonder, keeps himself in clouds,
And wants not buzzers to infect his ear
With pestilent speeches of his father's death;
Wherein necessity, of matter beggar'd,
Will nothing stick our person to arraign
In ear and ear.[500] O my dear Gertrude, this,
Like to a murdering-piece,[501] in many places
Gives me superfluous death. [*A noise within.*]
QUEEN. Alack, what noise is this?
KING. Where are my Switzers?[502] Let them guard the door.

[*Enter a* GENTLEMAN.]

What is the matter?
GENTLEMAN. Save yourself, my lord:
The ocean, overpeering of his list,[503]
Eats not the flats with more impetuous haste
Than young Laertes, in a riotous head,
O'erbears your officers. The rabble call him lord;
And, as[504] the world were now but to begin,
Antiquity forgot, custom not known,
The ratifiers and props of every word,
They cry 'Choose we: Laertes shall be king:'
Caps, hands, and tongues, applaud it to the clouds:
'Laertes shall be king, Laertes king!'
QUEEN. How cheerfully on the false trail they cry!
O, this is counter,[505] you false Danish dogs!
KING. The doors are broke. [*Noise within.*]

[*Enter* LAERTES, *armed;* DANES *following.*]

LAERTES. Where is this king? Sirs, stand you all without.

---

[500] "In *ear* and *ear*" is used, apparently, to give a plural sense.

[501] A murdering-piece, or *murderer*, was a small piece of artillery. Case-shot, filled with small bullets, nails, old iron, &c, was often used in these *murderers*. This accounts for the raking fire attributed to them in the text.

[502] *Switzers* for royal guards. The Swiss were then, as since, mercenary soldiers of any nation that could afford to pay them.

[503] *Overflowing* his *bounds*, or *limits.*

[504] *As* has here the force of *as if.* The explanation sometimes given of the passage is, that the rabble are the ratifiers and props of every *idle* word. The plain sense is, that antiquity and custom are the ratifiers and props of every *sound* word touching the matter in hand, the ordering of human society, and the State.

[505] Hounds are said to run *counter* when they are upon a false scent, or hunt by the heel, running backward and mistaking the course of the game.

DANES. No, let's come in.
LAERTES. I pray you, give me leave.
DANES. We will, we will. [*They retire without the door.*]
LAERTES. I thank you: keep the door. O thou vile king,
    Give me my father!
QUEEN. Calmly, good Laertes.
LAERTES. That drop of blood that's calm proclaims me bastard,
    Cries cuckold to my father, brands the harlot
    Even here, between the chaste unsmirchèd[506] brow
    Of my true mother.
KING. What is the cause, Laertes,
    That thy rebellion looks so giant-like?
    Let him go, Gertrude; do not fear our person:
    There's such divinity doth hedge a king,
    That treason can but peep to what it would,
    Acts little of his will. Tell me, Laertes,
    Why thou art thus incensed. Let him go, Gertrude.
    Speak, man.
LAERTES. Where is my father?
KING. Dead.
QUEEN. But not by him.
KING. Let him demand his fill.
LAERTES. How came he dead? I'll not be juggled with:
    To hell, allegiance! vows, to the blackest devil!
    Conscience and grace, to the profoundest pit!
    I dare damnation. To this point I stand,
    That both the worlds I give to negligence,
    Let come what comes; only I'll be reveng'd
    Most thoroughly[507] for my father.
KING. Who shall stay you?
LAERTES. My will, not all the world:
    And for my means, I'll husband them so well,
    They shall go far with little.
KING. Good Laertes,
    If you desire to know the certainty
    Of your dear father's death, is't writ in your revenge,
    That, swoopstake,[508] you will draw both friend and foe,
    Winner and loser?
LAERTES. None but his enemies.
KING. Will you know them then?

---

[506] *Unsmirched* is *unsullied, spotless.*

[507] *Throughly* and *thoroughly*, as also *through* and *thorough*, were used indifferently in the Poet's time.

[508] *Swoopstake* here means *indiscriminately.* A sweepstake is one who wins or *sweeps in all the stakes*, whether on the race-grounds or at the gaming-table.

LAERTES. To his good friends thus wide I'll ope my arms;
    And like the kind life-rendering pelican,
    Repast them with my blood.[509]
KING. Why, now you speak
    Like a good child and a true gentleman.
    That I am guiltless of your father's death,
    And am most sensible in grief for it,
    It shall as level to your judgment pierce[510]
    As day does to your eye.
    [*Within.*] Let her come in.
LAERTES. How now! what noise is that?

    [*Re-enter* OPHELIA.]

    O heat, dry up my brains! tears seven times salt,
    Burn out the sense and virtue of mine eye!
    By heaven, thy madness shall be paid by weight,
    Till our scale turn the beam. O rose of May!
    Dear maid, kind sister, sweet Ophelia!
    O heavens! is't possible, a young maid's wits
    Should be as moral as an old man's life?
    Nature is fine in love, and where 'tis fine,
    It sends some precious instance of itself
    After the thing it loves.[511]
OPHELIA. [*Sings.*]

        'They bore him barefaced on the bier;
          Hey non nonny, nonny, hey nonny;
        And in his grave rain'd many a tear'—

    Fare you well, my dove!
LAERTES. Hadst thou thy wits, and didst persuade revenge,
    It could not move thus.
OPHELIA. You must sing 'Down, a-down, an you call him a-down-a.'
    O, how the wheel[512] becomes it! It is the false steward, that stole

---

    [509] The pelican is a fabulous bird, often referred to by the old poets for illustration. An old book entitled *A Choice of Emblems and other Devices*, by Geffrey Whitney, 1586, contains a picture of an eagle on her nest, tearing open her breast to feed her young.

    [510] *Level*, again, for *direct.—Pierce*, here, has the sense of *penetrate*, that is, *go through* or *reach*.

    [511] Here, as often, *instance* is *proof, example*, specimen, *assurance*. The precious thing which Ophelia's fineness of nature has sent after her father is "her fair judgment," that is, her sanity.

    [512] The *wheel* is the *burden* of a ballad; from the Latin *rota*, a *round*, which is usually accompanied with a burden frequently repeated.

his master's daughter.[513]

LAERTES. This nothing's more than matter.[514]

OPHELIA. There's rosemary, that's for remembrance; pray, love, remember: and there is pansies. that's for thoughts.[515]

LAERTES. A document[516] in madness, thoughts and remembrance fitted.

OPHELIA. There's fennel for you, and columbines:[517] there's rue for you; and here's some for me: we may call it herb-grace o' Sundays: O you must wear your rue with a difference.[518] There's a daisy: I would give you some violets,[519] but they withered all when my father died: they say he made a good end.

[*Sings.*] 'For bonny sweet Robin is all my joy.'[520]

LAERTES. Thought and affliction, passion,[521] hell itself, She turns to favour and to prettiness.

OPHELIA. [*Sings.*]

---

[513] Probably some old ballad, of which no traces have come to light.

[514] He means that Ophelia's nonsense tells more, as to her condition, than speaking sense would.

[515] The language of flowers is very ancient, and the old poets have many instances of it. In *The Winter's Tale*, iv. 3, Perdita makes herself delectable in the use of it, distributing her flowers much as Ophelia does here. Rosemary, being supposed to strengthen the memory, was held emblematic of remembrance, and in that thought was distributed at weddings and funerals.—Pansies, from the French *pensees*, were emblems of pensiveness, *thought* being here again used for *grief*. The next speech, "*thoughts* and remembrance fitted," is another instance.

[516] *Document*, from the Latin *doceo*, was often used in the original sense of *lesson*, or something *taught*. So in *The Faerie Queene*, i. 10, 19, where Fidelia takes the Redcross Knight under her tuition, and draws upon "her sacred booke,"

And heavenly *documents* thereout did preach,
That weaker witt of man could never reach.

[517] Fennel and columbine were significant of cajolery and ingratitude; so that Ophelia might fitly give them to the guileful and faithless King.

[518] Rue was emblematic of sorrow or *ruth*, and was called *herb-grace* from the moral and medicinal virtues ascribed to it.—There may be some uncertainty as to Ophelia's meaning, when she says to the Queen, "you must wear your rue with a difference." *Bearing a difference* is an old heraldic phrase; and the difference here intended is probably best explained in Cogan's *Haven of Health*: "The second property is that *rue abateth carnal lust*, which is also confirmed by Galen." So that the difference in the Queen's case would be emblematic of her "hasty return to the nuptial state, and a severe reflection on her indecent marriage."

[519] The daisy was an emblem of dissembling; the violet, of faithfulness, and is so set down in *The Lover s Nosegay*.

[520] Poor Ophelia in her madness remembers fragments of many old popular ballads. *Bonny Robin* appears to have been a favourite, for there were many others written to that tune.

[521] *Thought*, again, for *grief.*—*Passion* for *suffering*; the classical sense.

'And will he not come again?
And will he not come again?
No, no, he is dead:
Go to thy death-bed:
He never will come again.'

'His beard was as white as snow,
All flaxen was his poll:[522]
He is gone, he is gone,
And we cast away moan:
God ha' mercy on his soul!'

And of[523] all Christian souls, I pray God. God be wi' ye. [*Exit.*]
LAERTES. Do you see this, O God?
KING. Laertes, I must commune with your grief,
Or you deny me right. Go but apart,
Make choice of whom your wisest friends you will.
And they shall hear and judge 'twixt you and me.
If by direct or by collateral hand
They find us touch'd, we will our kingdom give,
Our crown, our life, and all that we can ours,
To you in satisfaction; but if not,
Be you content to lend your patience to us,
And we shall jointly labour with your soul
To give it due content.
LAERTES. Let this be so;
His means of death, his obscure funeral—
No trophy, sword, nor hatchment o'er his bones,
No noble rite nor formal ostentation[524]—
Cry to be heard, as 'twere from heaven to earth,
That I must call't in question.
KING. So you shall;
And where the offence is let the great axe fall.
I pray you, go with me. [*Exeunt.*]

---

[522] *Poll* was in common use for *head.* Relics of the old usage survive still in our *polls and poll-tax,* where men are counted and taxed by the head.

[523] *Of,* again, for *on.*

[524] The funerals of knights and persons of rank were made with great ceremony and ostentation formerly. Sir John Hawkins observes that "the sword, the helmet, the gauntlet, spurs, and tabard are still hung over the grave of every knight."

SCENE III.

The Same. Another Room in the Castle.

[*Enter* HORATIO *and a* SERVANT.]

HORATIO. What are they that would speak with me?
SERVANT. Sailors, sir: they say they have letters for you.
HORATIO. Let them come in. [*Exit* SERVANT.]
  I do not know from what part of the world
  I should be greeted, if not from Lord Hamlet.

[*Enter Sailors.*]

SAILOR. God bless you, sir.
HORATIO. Let him bless thee too.
SAILOR. He shall, sir, an't please him. There's a letter for you, sir; it comes from the ambassador that was bound for England; if your name be Horatio, as I am let to know it is.
HORATIO. [*Reads.*] 'Horatio, when thou shalt have overlooked this, give these fellows some means to the king: they have letters for him. Ere we were two days old at sea, a pirate of very warlike appointment[525] gave us chase. Finding ourselves too slow of sail, we put on a compelled valour, and in the grapple I boarded them: on the instant they got clear of our ship; so I alone became their prisoner. They have dealt with me like thieves of mercy: but they knew what they did; I am to do a good turn for them. Let the king have the letters I have sent; and repair thou to me with as much speed as thou wouldst fly death. I have words to speak in thine ear will make thee dumb; yet are they much too light for the bore[526] of the matter. These good fellows will bring thee where I am. Rosencrantz and Guildenstern hold their course for England: of them I have much to tell thee. Farewell.
      'He that thou knowest thine, HAMLET.'

  Come, I will make you way for these your letters;
  And do't the speedier, that you may direct me
  To him from whom you brought them. [*Exeunt.*]

---

[525] *Appointment*, here, is *armament*, or *equipment*. Still used thus in military language. Also in "a *well-appointed* house"; meaning, of course, *well-furnished*, or *well-ordered*.
[526] The *bore* is the *caliber* or *capacity* of a gun; as a ten-pounder, or a seventy-four pounder, according to the weight of the ball.

SCENE IV.

Another Room in the Castle.

[*Enter the* KING, *and* LAERTES.]

KING. Now must your conscience my acquaintance seal,
  And you must put me in your heart for friend,
  Sith you have heard, and with a knowing ear,
  That he which hath your noble father slain
  Pursued my life.
LAERTES. It well appears: but tell me
  Why you proceeded not against these feats,
  So crimeful and so capital in nature,
  As by your safety, wisdom, all things else,
  You mainly[527] were stirr'd up.
KING. O, for two special reasons;
  Which may to you, perhaps, seem much unsinew'd,
  But yet to me they are strong. The queen his mother
  Lives almost by his looks; and for myself—
  My virtue or my plague, be it either which—
  She's so conjunctive to my life and soul,
  That, as the star moves not but in his sphere,
  I could not but by her. The other motive,
  Why to a public count I might not go,
  Is the great love the general gender[528] bear him;
  Who, dipping all his faults in their affection,
  Work like the spring that turneth wood to stone,
  Convert his gyves to graces;[529] so that my arrows,
  Too slightly timber'd for so loud a wind,[530]
  Would have reverted to my bow again,
  And not where I had aim'd them.[531]
LAERTES. And so have I a noble father lost;
  A sister driven into desperate terms,
  Whose worth, if praises may go back again,[532]

---

[527] The Poet sometimes uses *mainly* for *greatly* or *strongly.* So in *Troilus and Cressida,* iv. 4: "I do not call your faith in question so *mainly* as my merit."

[528] "The general *gender*" is the common *race* or *sort* of people; the multitude. Shakespeare has the like phrase, "one *gender* of herbs."

[529] Punishment would invest him with more grace in the people's eye; his *fetters* would make him appear the lovelier to them.

[530] So in Roger Ascham's *Toxophilus:* "Weake bowes and lyghte shaftes cannot stande in a *rough* wynde."

[531] Elliptical. "And *would not have gone* where I had aim'd them."

[532] "If I may praise her for what she was, but has now ceased to be." Or, perhaps, "If

    Stood challenger on mount of all the age[533]
    For her perfections: but my revenge will come.
KING. Break not your sleeps for that: you must not think
    That we are made of stuff so flat and dull
    That we can let our beard be shook with danger
    And think it pastime. You shortly shall hear more:
    I loved your father, and we love ourself;
    And that, I hope, will teach you to imagine—

[Enter a Messenger.]

    How now! what news?
MESSENGER. Letters, my lord, from Hamlet:
    This to your majesty; this to the queen.
KING. From Hamlet! who brought them?
MESSENGER. Sailors, my lord, they say; I saw them not:
    They were given me by Claudio; he received them
    Of him that brought them.
KING. Laertes, you shall hear them. Leave us. *[Exit Messenger.]*

    [Reads.] 'High and mighty, You shall know I am set naked[534] on your kingdom. To-morrow shall I beg leave to see your kingly eyes: when I shall, first asking your pardon thereunto, recount the occasion of my sudden and more strange return.' HAMLET.

    What should this mean? Are all the rest come back?
    Or is it some abuse,[535] and no such thing?
LAERTES. Know you the hand?
KING. 'Tis Hamlets character. 'Naked!'
    And in a postscript here, he says 'alone.'
    Can you advise me?
LAERTES. I'm lost in it, my lord. But let him come;
    It warms the very sickness in my heart,
    That I shall live and tell him to his teeth,
    'Thus didest thou.'
KING. If it be so, Laertes—
    As how should it be so? how otherwise?[536]—
    Will you be ruled by me?

I may go back to her as a theme of praise."
   [533] That is, "stood challenger of all the age."
   [534] *Naked*, here, means destitute of attendants; *alone.*
   [535] *Abuse* for *cheat, deception,* or *delusion.* Often so.
   [536] That is, "how should it be either true or not true?" The thing seems incredible either way; incredible that Hamlet should have returned; incredible that the letter should not be in Hamlet's *character,* or *hand-writing.*

LAERTES. Ay, my lord;
   So you will not o'errule me to a peace.
KING. To thine own peace. If he be now return'd,
   As checking[537] at his voyage, and that he means
   No more to undertake it, I will work him
   To an exploit, now ripe in my device,
   Under the which he shall not choose but fall:
   And for his death no wind of blame shall breathe,
   But even his mother shall uncharge the practise[538]
   And call it accident.
LAERTES. My lord, I will be ruled;
   The rather, if you could devise it so
   That I might be the organ.
KING. It falls right.
   You have been talk'd of since your travel much,
   And that in Hamlet's hearing, for a quality
   Wherein, they say, you shine: your sum of parts
   Did not together pluck such envy from him
   As did that one, and that, in my regard,
   Of the unworthiest siege.[539]
LAERTES. What part is that, my lord?
KING. A very[540] riband in the cap of youth,
   Yet needful too; for youth no less becomes
   The light and careless livery that it wears
   Than settled age his sables and his weeds,
   Importing health and graveness.[541] Two months since,
   Here was a gentleman of Normandy—
   I've seen myself, and served against, the French,
   And they can[542] well on horseback: but this gallant
   Had witchcraft in't; he grew unto his seat;
   And to such wondrous doing brought his horse,
   As he had been incorps'd and demi-natured
   With the brave beast: so far he topp'd my thought,
   That I, in forgery of shapes and tricks,[543]

---

[537] To *check at* is a term in falconry, meaning to start away or fly off from the lure. So in Hinde's *Eliosto Libidinoso*, 1606: "For who knows not, quoth she, that this hawk, which comes now so fair to the fist, may to-morrow *check at* the lure?"

[538] *Acquit* the proceeding or the *contrivance* of all *design.*

[539] The Poet again uses *siege* for *seat*, that is, *place* or *rank*, in *Othello*, i. 2: "I fetch my life and being from men of royal siege." The usage was not uncommon.

[540] The Poet repeatedly has *very* in the sense of *mere.*

[541] The sense of *health* goes with the preceding clause; the "light and careless livery" denoting health, as the black dress denotes gravity.—*Weeds* was used for *clothes* or *dress* in general. Here the sense of *settled* continues over *weeds: staid* or *sober* dress

[542] *Can* is here used in its original sense of *ability* or *skill.*

[543] That is, in *the imagination* of shapes and tricks, or *feats.* This use of *forge* and

Come short of what he did.
LAERTES. A Norman was't?
KING. A Norman.
LAERTES. Upon my life, Lamond.
KING. The very same.
LAERTES. I know him well: he is the brooch,[544] indeed,
And gem of all the nation.
KING. He made confession of you,
And gave you such a masterly report
For art and exercise in your defence[545]
And for your rapier most especially,
That he cried out, 'twould be a sight indeed,
If one could match you: the scrimers[546] of their nation,
He swore, had had neither motion, guard, nor eye,
If you opposed them. Sir, this report of his
Did Hamlet so envenom with his envy,[547]
That he could nothing do but wish and beg
Your sudden coming o'er, to play with him.
Now, out of this—
LAERTES. What out of this, my lord?
KING. Laertes, was your father dear to you?
Or are you like the painting of a sorrow,
A face without a heart?
LAERTES. Why ask you this?
KING. Not that I think you did not love your father;
But that I know love is begun by time;[548]
And that I see, in passages of proof,[549]
Time qualifies the spark and fire of it.
There lives within the very flame of love
A kind of wick or snuff that will abate it;
And nothing is at a like goodness still;
For goodness, growing to a plurisy,[550]

---

forgery was not unfrequent.—To *top* is to *surpass.*

[544] *Brooch* for any conspicuous ornament. So in *The World runnes on Wheeles,* 1630: "These sonnes of Mars, who in their times were the glorious *Brooches* of our nation, and admirable terrour to our enemies."

[545] *Defence* here means *fencing* or *sword-practice.*

[546] *Scrimer* is from the French *escrimeur,* which means *fencer.*

[547] "With envy *of you.*" The objective genitive, as it is called. Shakespeare often has both the objective and the subjective genitive in cases where present usage does not admit them.

[548] As love is begun by *time,* and has its gradual increase, so *time* qualifies and abates it.

[549] *Passages of proof* means *instances of trial,* or *experience.*

[550] *Plurisy* is from the Latin *plus, pluris,* and must not be confounded with *pleurisy.* It means *excess,* much the same as Burns's "*unco guid.*" So in Massinger's *Unnatural Combat:* "*Plurisy* of goodness is thy ill."

Dies in his own too much: that we would do
We should do when we would; for this 'would' changes
And hath abatements and delays as many
As there are tongues, are hands, are accidents;
And then this 'should' is like a spendthrift sigh,
That hurts by easing.[551] But, to the quick o' the ulcer:
Hamlet comes back: what would you undertake,
To show yourself your father's son in deed
More than in words?

LAERTES. To cut his throat i' the church.

KING. No place, indeed, should murder sanctuarize;[552]
Revenge should have no bounds. But, good Laertes,
Will you do this,[553] keep close within your chamber.
Hamlet return'd shall know you are come home:
We'll put on[554] those shall praise your excellence
And set a double varnish on the fame
The Frenchman gave you, bring you in fine together
And wager on your heads: he, being remiss,
Most generous and free from all contriving,
Will not peruse[555] the foils; so that, with ease,
Or with a little shuffling, you may choose
A sword unbated,[556] and in a pass of practise
Requite him for your father.

LAERTES. I will do't;
And, for that purpose, I'll anoint my sword.
I bought an unction of a mountebank,[557]
So mortal that, but dip a knife in it,
Where it draws blood no cataplasm[558] so rare,

---

[551] It was anciently believed that sighing consumed the blood. The Poet has several allusions to this. There is also a fine moral meaning in the figure. Jeremy Taylor speaks of certain people who take to a sentimental penitence, as "cozening themselves with their own tears," as if these would absolve them from "doing works meet for repentence." Such tears may be fitly said to "hurt by easing."

[552] Murder should not have the protection or privilege of sanctuary in any place. The allusion is to the rights of sanctuary with which certain religious places were formerly invested, so that criminals resorting to them were shielded not only from private revenge, but from the arm of the law.

[553] That is, "*If you* will do this"; or, "If you *would* do this."

[554] *Put on*, here, is *stir up*, *incite*, or, as we say, *set on*.

[555] *Peruse*, for *observe closely* or *scrutinize*.

[556] *Unbated* is *unblunted*: a foil without the cap, or button, which was put upon the point, when fencers were to play or practise their art.—*A pass of practice* is a *thrust* made as in exercise of skill; the thruster pretending to be ignorant of the button's being off the foil.

[557] *Mountebank* commonly meant a *quack*, but is here put, apparently, for *druggist* or *apothecary*. The word seems to have been used originally of a pedlar or pretender who mounted a bench, or a bank by the wayside, and hawked off his wares or his skill.—Here, as generally in Shakespeare, *mortal* is *deadly*; that which *kills*.

Collected from all simples that have virtue
Under the moon, can save the thing from death
That is but scratch'd withal: I'll touch my point
With this contagion, that, if I gall him slightly,
It may be death.
KING. Let's further think of this;
Weigh what convenience both of time and means
May fit us to our shape: if this should fail,
And that our drift look through our bad performance,[559]
'Twere better not assay'd, therefore this project
Should have a back or second, that might hold,
If this should blast in proof.[560] Soft! let me see.
We'll make a solemn wager on your cunnings—I ha't.
When in your motion you are hot and dry—
As make your bouts more violent to that end—
And that he calls for drink, I'll have prepared him
A chalice for the nonce,[561] whereon but sipping,
If he by chance escape your venom'd stuck,[562]
Our purpose may hold there.

[*Enter the* QUEEN.]

How no, sweet Queen!
QUEEN. One woe doth tread upon another's heel,
So fast they follow; your sister's drown'd, Laertes.
LAERTES. Drown'd! O, where?[563]
QUEEN. There is a willow grows aslant a brook,
That shows his hoar leaves in the glassy stream;
There with fantastic garlands did she come
Of crow-flowers, nettles, daisies, and long purples
That liberal[564] shepherds give a grosser name,

---

[558] *Cataplasm* is a *soft plaster,* or a *poultice.*—*Simples* is, properly, *herbs;* but was used of any *medicine.*

[559] "If our purpose should expose or betray itself through lack of skill in the execution."

[560] Should break down in the trial. The image is of proving guns, which of course sometimes burst in the testing.

[561] "For the *nonce*" is for the *occasion;* literally, for the *once.*

[562] *Stuck,* a fencing-term, is *thrust;* the same as the Italian and Spanish *stoccata* and *staccado.* So in *Twelfth Night,* iii. 4: "He gives me the *stuck-in* with such mortal motion, that it is inevitable."

[563] That Laertes might be excused in some degree for not cooling, the Act concludes with the affecting death of Ophelia; who in the beginning lay like a little projection of land into a lake or stream, covered with spray-flowers, quietly reflected in the quiet waters; but at length is undermined or loosened, and becomes a fairy isle, and after a brief vagrancy sinks almost without an eddy.—COLERIDGE.

[564] *Liberal* is repeatedly used by Shakespeare for *loose-tongued.*

But our cold maids do dead men's fingers call them:
There, on the pendent boughs her coronet weeds
Clambering to hang, an envious sliver broke;
When down her weedy trophies and herself
Fell in the weeping brook. Her clothes spread wide;
And, mermaid-like, awhile they bore her up:
Which time she chanted snatches of old tunes;
As one incapable[565] of her own distress,
Or like a creature native and endued
Unto that element: but long it could not be
Till that her garments, heavy with their drink,
Pull'd the poor wretch[566] from her melodious lay
To muddy death.
LAERTES. Alas, then, she is drown'd?
QUEEN. Drown'd, drown'd.
LAERTES. Too much of water hast thou, poor Ophelia,
    And therefore I forbid my tears: but yet
    It is our trick; nature her custom holds,
    Let shame say what it will: when these are gone,
    The woman will be out.[567] Adieu, my lord:
    I have a speech of fire, that fain would blaze,
    But that this folly douts it. [*Exit.*]
KING. Let's follow, Gertrude:
    How much I had to do to calm his rage!
    Now fear I this will give it start again;
    Therefore let's follow. [*Exeunt.*]

---

[565] *Incapable* for *insensible* or *unconscious.* The Poet has it so in one or two other places.

[566] *Wretch,* again, as a strong term of endearment.

[567] "I shall have wept the woman's tenderness all out of me, and shall be again ready for a man's work."

ACT V.

SCENE I.

Elsinore. A Churchyard.

[*Enter two Clowns, with spades, &c.*]

FIRST CLOWN. Is she to be buried in Christian burial that wilfully seeks her own salvation?

SECOND CLOWN. I tell thee she is: and therefore make her grave straight:[568] the crowner hath sat on her, and finds it Christian burial.

FIRST CLOWN. How can that be, unless she drowned herself in her own defence?

SECOND CLOWN. Why, 'tis found so.

FIRST CLOWN. It must be 'se offendendo;'[569] it cannot be else. For here lies the point: if I drown myself wittingly, it argues an act: and an act hath three branches: it is, to act, to do, to perform; argal,[570] she drowned herself wittingly.

SECOND CLOWN. Nay, but hear you, Goodman delver—

FIRST CLOWN. Give me leave. Here lies the water; good: here stands the man; good; if the man go to this water, and drown himself, it is, will he, nill he,[571] he goes,—mark you that; but if the water come to him and drown him, he drowns not himself: argal, he that is not guilty of his own death shortens not his own life.

SECOND CLOWN. But is this law?

FIRST CLOWN. Ay, marry, is't; crowner's quest law.[572]

SECOND CLOWN. Will you ha' the truth on't? If this had not been a gentlewoman, she should have been buried out o' Christian burial.

FIRST CLOWN. Why, there thou say'st: and the more pity that great folk should have countenance in this world to drown or hang

---

[568] *Straight* for *straightway* or *immediately*; a common usage.

[569] The Clown, in undertaking to show off his legal learning, blunders *offendendo* for *defendendo.*

[570] *Argal* is an old vulgar corruption of the Latin *ergo, therefore.*

[571] "Will he, *nill* he," is will he, *or will* he *not.*

[572] Hawkins thinks the Poet here meant to ridicule a case reported by Plowden. Sir James Hales had drowned himself in a fit of insanity, and the legal question was whether his lease was thereby forfeited. Much subtilty was expended in finding out whether Sir James was the *agent* or the *patient*; that is, whether *he went to the water* or *the water came to him.* The following is part of the argument: "Sir James Hales was dead, and how came he to his death? It may be answered, by drowning; and who drowned him? Sir James Hales; and when did he drown him? In his lifetime. So that Sir James Hales being alive caused Sir James Hales to die, and the act of the living man was the death of the dead man."

themselves, more than their even Christian.[573] Come, my spade. There is no ancient gentleman but gardeners, ditchers, and grave-makers: they hold up Adam's profession.

SECOND CLOWN. Was he a gentleman?

FIRST CLOWN. He was the first that ever bore arms.

SECOND CLOWN. Why, he had none.

FIRST CLOWN. What, art a heathen? How dost thou understand the Scripture? The Scripture says 'Adam digg'd.' Could he dig without arms? I'll put another question to thee: if thou answerest me not to the purpose, confess thyself—

SECOND CLOWN. Go to.

FIRST CLOWN. What is he that builds stronger than either the mason, the shipwright, or the carpenter?

SECOND CLOWN. The gallows-maker; for that frame outlives a thousand tenants.

FIRST CLOWN. I like thy wit well, in good faith: the gallows does well; but how does it well? it does well to those that do in: now thou dost ill to say the gallows is built stronger than the church: argal, the gallows may do well to thee. To't again, come.

SECOND CLOWN. 'Who builds stronger than a mason, a shipwright, or a carpenter?'

FIRST CLOWN. Ay, tell me that, and unyoke.[574]

SECOND CLOWN. Marry, now I can tell.

FIRST CLOWN. To't.

SECOND CLOWN. Mass, I cannot tell.

[*Enter* HAMLET *and* HORATIO, *at some distance.*]

FIRST CLOWN. Cudgel thy brains no more about it, for your dull ass will not mend his pace with beating; and, when you are asked this question next, say 'a grave-maker: the houses that he makes last till doomsday. Go, get thee to Yaughan; fetch me a stoup of liquor. [*Exit* SECOND CLOWN.]

[*Digs and sings.*]

'In youth, when I did love, did love,
    Methought it was very sweet,
To contract, O, the time, for, ah, my behoove,
    O, methought, there was nothing meet.'[575]

---

[573] *Even-Christian* for *fellow-Christian*; an old expression, to be found in Chaucer. Wicliffe has *even-servant* for *fellow-servant.*

[574] This was a common phrase for giving over or ceasing to do a thing; a metaphor derived from the *unyoking* of oxen at the end of their labour.

[575] The original ballad from whence these stanzas are taken is printed in Tottel's

HAMLET. Has this fellow no feeling of his business, that he sings at grave-making?

HORATIO. Custom hath made it in him a property of easiness.

HAMLET. 'Tis e'en so: the hand of little employment hath the daintier sense.

FIRST CLOWN. [*Sings.*]

> 'But age, with his stealing steps,
> Hath claw'd me in his clutch,
> And hath shipped me into the land,
> As if I had never been such.' [*Throws up a skull.*]

HAMLET. That skull had a tongue in it, and could sing once: how the knave jowls it to the ground, as if it were Cain's jaw-bone, that did the first murder! It might be the pate of a politician, which this ass now o'er-reaches; one that would circumvent God, might it not?[576]

HORATIO. It might, my lord.

HAMLET. Or of a courtier; which could say 'Good morrow, sweet lord! How dost thou, good lord?' This might be my lord such-a-one, that praised my lord such-a-one's horse, when he meant to beg it; might it not?

HORATIO. Ay, my lord.

HAMLET. Why, e'en so: and now my Lady Worm's;[577] chapless, and knocked about the mazzard with a sexton's spade: here's fine revolution, an we had the trick to see't. Did these bones cost no more the breeding, but to play at loggats[578] with 'em? Mine ache to think on't.

Miscellany, or Songes and Sonnettes by Lord Surrey and others, 1575. The ballad is attributed to Lord Vaux, and is printed by Dr. Percy in his *Reliques of Ancient Poetry.* The *O's* and *ahs* are meant to express the Clown's gruntings as he digs.

[576] Shakespeare uses *politician* for a *plotter* or *schemer*; one who is ever trying to out-craft and overreach his neighbour, and even Providence, and to intrigue his way to popularity or profit. The equivoque in *o'erreaches* is obvious enough.

[577] The skull that was *my Lord Such-a-one's* is now *my Lady Worm's.*

[578] *Loggats* are small logs or pieces of wood. Hence *loggats* was the name of an ancient rustic game, wherein a stake was fixed in the ground at which *loggats* were thrown; in short, a ruder kind of quoit-play.

FIRST CLOWN. [*Sings.*]

> 'A pick-axe, and a spade, a spade,
> For and[579] a shrouding sheet:
> O, a pit of clay for to be made
> For such a guest is meet.'

[*Throws up another skull.*]

HAMLET. There's another: why may not that be the skull of a lawyer? Where be his quiddities now, his quillets,[580] his cases, his tenures, and his tricks? why does he suffer this rude knave now to knock him about the sconce[581] with a dirty shovel, and will not tell him of his action of battery? Hum! This fellow might be in's time a great buyer of land, with his statutes, his recognizances, his fines, his double vouchers, his recoveries:[582] is this the fine of his fines, and the recovery of his recoveries, to have his fine pate full of fine dirt?[583] will his vouchers vouch him no more of his purchases, and double ones too, than the length and breadth of a pair of indentures?[584] The very conveyances of his lands will hardly lie in this box; and must the inheritor himself have no more, ha?

HORATIO. Not a jot more, my lord.

---

[579] "*For and*," says Dyce, "in the present version of the stanza, answers to *And eke* in that given by Percy." So in Beaumont and Fletcher's *Knight of the Burning Pestle*: "Your squire doth come, and with him comes the lady, *for and* the Squire of Damsels, as I take it."

[580] *Quiddits* are quirks, or subtle questions; and *quillets* are nice and frivolous distinctions. The etymology of this last word has plagued many learned heads. Blount, in his *Glossography*, clearly points out *quodlibet* as the origin of it. Bishop Wilkins calls a *quillet* "a frivolousness."

[581] *Sconce* was not unfrequently used for *head.*

[582] Shakespeare here is profuse of his legal learning. Ritson, a lawyer, shall interpret for him: "A recovery with *double voucher* is so called from *two* persons being successively *voucher*, or called upon to warrant the tenant's title. Both *fines* and *recoveries* are fictions of law, used to convert an estate tail into a fee-simple. Statutes are (not acts of parliament but) statutes *merchant* and staple, particular modes of *recognizance* or acknowledgment for securing *debts*, which thereby become a charge upon the party's land. *Statutes* and *recognizances* are constantly mentioned together in the covenants of a purchase deed."

[583] Here we have *fine* used in four different senses: first, in the proper Latin sense, *end*; second, in the legal sense, to denote certain processes in law; third, in the sense of *proud, elegant,* or *refined*; fourth, in the ordinary sense of *small.*

[584] *Indenture, conveyance,* and *assurance* are all used here as equivalent terms, and mean what we call *deeds*; instruments relating to the tenure and transfer of property. They were called *indentures*, because two copies were written on the same sheet of parchment, which was cut in two in a toothed or *indented* line, to guard against counterfeits, and to prove genuineness in case of controversy.—*Inheritor*, in the next line, is *possessor* or *owner*. The Poet often uses the verb to *inherit* in the same sense.

HAMLET. Is not parchment made of sheepskins?

HORATIO. Ay, my lord, and of calf-skins too.

HAMLET. They are sheep and calves which seek out assurance in that.[585] I will speak to this fellow. Whose grave's this, sirrah?

FIRST CLOWN. Mine, sir.

> [*Sings.*]   'O, a pit of clay for to be made
> For such a guest is meet.'

HAMLET. I think it be thine, indeed; for thou liest in't.

FIRST CLOWN. You lie out on't, sir, and therefore it is not yours: for my part, I do not lie in't, and yet it is mine.

HAMLET. 'Thou dost lie in't, to be in't and say it is thine: 'tis for the dead, not for the quick; therefore thou liest.

FIRST CLOWN. 'Tis a quick lie, sir; 'twill away gain, from me to you.

HAMLET. What man dost thou dig it for?

FIRST CLOWN. For no man, sir.

HAMLET. What woman, then?

FIRST CLOWN. For none, neither.

HAMLET. Who is to be buried in't?

FIRST CLOWN. One that was a woman, sir; but, rest her soul, she's dead.

HAMLET. How absolute the knave is! we must speak by the card,[586] or equivocation will undo us. By the Lord, Horatio, these three years I have taken a note of it; the age is grown so pickèd[587] that the toe of the peasant comes so near the heel of the courtier, he gaffs his kibe.[588] How long hast thou been a grave-maker?

FIRST CLOWN. Of all the days i' the year, I came to't that day that our last king Hamlet overcame Fortinbras.

HAMLET. How long is that since?

FIRST CLOWN. Cannot you tell that? Every fool can tell that: it was the very day that young Hamlet was born; he that is mad, and sent into England.

HAMLET. Ay, marry, why was he sent into England?

FIRST CLOWN. Why, because he was mad: he shall recover his wits there; or, if he do not, it's no great matter there.

HAMLET. Why?

FIRST CLOWN. 'Twill, a not be seen in him there; there the men are as mad as he.

---

[585] A quibble is here implied upon *parchment*; deeds, which were always written on parchment, being in legal language "common assurances."

[586] To speak by the card, is to speak precisely, by rule, or according to a prescribed course. It is a metaphor from the seaman's *card* or chart by which he guides his course.

[587] *Picked* is *curious, over-nice*.

[588] *Kibe* is an old word for *chilblain*. The Poet has it several times.

HAMLET. How came he mad?

FIRST CLOWN. Very strangely, they say.

HAMLET. How strangely?

FIRST CLOWN. Faith, e'en with losing his wits.

HAMLET. Upon what ground?

FIRST CLOWN. Why, here in Denmark: I have been sexton here, man and boy, thirty years.

HAMLET. How long will a man lie i' the earth ere he rot?

FIRST CLOWN. Faith, if 'a be not rotten before 'a die—as we have many pocky corpses now-a-days, that will scarce hold the laying in—'a will last you some eight year or nine year: a tanner will last you nine year.

HAMLET. Why he more than another?

FIRST CLOWN. Why, sir, his hide is so tanned with his trade, that he will keep out water a great while; and your water is a sore decayer of your whoreson dead body. Here's a skull now; this skull has lain in the earth three and twenty years.

HAMLET. Whose was it?

FIRST CLOWN. A whoreson mad fellow's it was: whose do you think it was?

HAMLET. Nay, I know not.

FIRST CLOWN. A pestilence on him for a mad rogue! a' poured a flagon of Rhenish on my head once. This same skull, sir, was Yorick's skull, the king's jester.

HAMLET. This?

FIRST CLOWN. E'en that.

HAMLET. Let me see. [*Takes the skull.*] Alas, poor Yorick! I knew him, Horatio: a fellow of infinite jest, of most excellent fancy: he hath borne me on his back a thousand times; and now, how abhorred in my imagination it is! my gorge rims at it. Here hung those lips that I have kissed I know not how oft. Where be your gibes now? Your gambols? your songs? your flashes of merriment, that were wont to set the table on a roar? Not one now, to mock your own grinning? quite chap-fallen? Now get you to my lady's chamber, and tell her, let her paint an inch thick, to this favour she must come; make her laugh at that. Prithee, Horatio, tell me one thing.

HORATIO. What's that, my lord?

HAMLET. Dost thou think Alexander looked o' this fashion i' the earth?

HORATIO. E'en so.

HAMLET. And smelt so? Pah! [*Puts down the skull.*]

HORATIO. E'en so, my lord.

HAMLET. To what base uses we may return, Horatio! Why may not
imagination trace the noble dust of Alexander, till he find it
stopping a bung-hole?

HORATIO. 'Twere to consider too curiously, to consider so.

HAMLET. No, faith, not a jot; but to follow him thither with modesty
enough, and likelihood to lead it: as thus: Alexander died,
Alexander was buried, Alexander returneth into dust; the dust is
earth; of earth we make loam; and why of that loam, whereto he
was converted, might they not stop a beer-barrel?

> Imperious Caesar, dead and turn'd to clay,
> Might stop a hole to keep the wind away:
> O, that that earth, which kept the world in awe,
> Should patch a wall to expel the winter flaw![589]

But soft! but soft! aside: here comes the king.
The queen, the courtiers:

[*Enter* PRIESTS, *&c., in procession; the corpse of* OPEHLIA;
LAERTES *and* MOURNERS *following; the* KING, *the*
QUEEN, *their Trains, &c.*]

> Who is this they follow?
> And with such maimed rites? This doth betoken
> The corpse they follow did with desperate hand
> Fordo its own life: 'twas of some estate.[590]
> Couch we awhile, and mark. [*Retiring with* HORATIO.]

LAERTES. What ceremony else?

HAMLET. That is Laertes,
A very noble youth: mark.

LAERTES. What ceremony else?

PRIEST. Her obsequies have been as far enlarged
As we have warrantise. Her death was doubtful;
And, but that great command o'ersways the order,
She should in ground unsanctified have lodged
Till the last trumpet: for charitable prayers,
Shards,[591] flints and pebbles should be thrown on her;
Yet here she is allow'd her virgin crants,[592]

---

[589] A *flaw* is a violent gust or blast of wind.

[590] *Estate* was a common term for persons of *rank.*—To *fordo* is to *undo* or *destroy.*

[591] *Shards* not only means fragments of pots and tiles, but rubbish of any kind. Our version of the Bible has preserved to us *pot-sherds;* and bricklayers, in Surrey and Sussex, use the compounds *tile-sherds, slate-sherds.*—*For*, in the preceding line, has the force of *instead of.*

[592] *Crants* is an old word for *garlands;* very rare, and not used again by Shakespeare. It was customary in some parts of England to have a garland of flowers and sweet herbs carried before a maiden's coffin. Johnson says it was the custom in rural parishes in his time.

Her maiden strewments and the bringing home
Of[593] bell and burial.
LAERTES. Must there no more be done?
PRIEST. No more be done:
We should profane the service of the dead
To sing a requiem and such rest to her
As to peace-parted souls.[594]
LAERTES. Lay her i' the earth:
And from her fair and unpolluted flesh
May violets spring! I tell thee, churlish priest,
A ministering angel shall my sister be,
When thou liest howling.
HAMLET. What, the fair Ophelia!
QUEEN. Sweets to the sweet: farewell! [*Scattering flowers.*]
I hoped thou shouldst have been my Hamlet's wife;
I thought thy bride-bed to have deck'd, sweet maid,
And not have strew'd thy grave.
LAERTES. O, treble woe
Fall ten times treble on that cursèd head,
Whose wicked deed thy most ingenious[595] sense
Deprived thee of! Hold off the earth awhile,
Till I have caught her once more in mine arms:

[*Leaps into the grave.*]

Now pile your dust upon the quick and dead,
Till of this flat a mountain you have made,
To o'er-top old Pelion, or the skyish head
Of blue Olympus.
HAMLET. [*Advancing.*] What is he whose grief
Bears such an emphasis, whose phrase of sorrow
Conjures the wandering stars, and makes them stand
Like wonder-wounded hearers? This is I,
Hamlet the Dane. [*Leaps into the grave.*]
LAERTES. The devil take thy soul! [*Grappling with him.*]
HAMLET. Thou pray'st not well.
I prithee, take thy fingers from my throat;
For, though I am not splenitive and rash,

---

[593] *Of* has here the force of *with.*

[594] A *requiem* is a mass sung for the rest of the soul. So called from the words, *Requiem aeternam dona eis, Domine.*—"Peace-parted souls" is souls that have *departed in peace*; or, as the Prayer-book has it, "in favour with Thee our God, and in perfect charity with the world."

[595] *Ingenious* for *ingenuous, guileless.* Defoe has it so in his *Colonel Jack*, 1738: "But 'tis contrary to an *ingenious* spirit to delight in such service."

Yet have I something in me dangerous,
Which let thy wiseness fear: hold off thy hand.
KING. Pluck them asunder.
QUEEN. Hamlet, Hamlet!
ALL. Gentlemen!
HORATIO. Good my lord, be quiet.

[*The* ATTENDANTS *part them, and they come out of the grave.*]

HAMLET. Why I will fight with him upon this theme
Until my eyelids will no longer wag.
QUEEN. O my son, what theme?
HAMLET. I loved Ophelia: forty thousand brothers
Could not, with all their quantity of love,
Make up my sum. What wilt thou do for her?
KING. O, he is mad, Laertes.
QUEEN. For love of God, forbear him.
HAMLET. 'Swounds, show me what th'owt do:
Woo't weep, woo't fight, woo't fast, woo't tear thyself?
Woo't drink up Esill?[596] eat a crocodile?
I'll do't. Dost thou come here to whine?
To outface me with leaping in her grave?
Be buried quick[597] with her, and so will I:
And, if thou prate of mountains, let them throw
Millions of acres on us, till our ground,
Singeing his pate against the burning zone,[598]
Make Ossa like a wart! Nay, an thou'lt mouth,
I'll rant as well as thou.
QUEEN. This is mere[599] madness;
And thus awhile the fit will work on him;
Anon, as patient as the female dove,
When that her golden couplets are disclosed,[600]

---

[596] What particular lake, river, frith, or gulf was meant by the Poet, is something uncertain. The more common opinion is, that he had in mind the river *Yesel*, which, of the larger branches of the Rhine, is the one nearest to Denmark. In the maps of our time, *Isef* is the name of a gulf almost surrounded by land, in the Island of Zealand, not many miles west of Elsinore. Either of these names might naturally enough have been spelt and pronounced *Esill* or *hell* by an Englishman in Shakespeare's time. In strains of hyperbole, such figures of speech were often used by the old poets.—*Woo't* is a contraction of *wouldst thou*, said to be common in the northern counties of England.

[597] *Quick* in its old sense of *alive*, as in the Nicene Creed. The Poet has it repeatedly so.

[598] "The burning zone" is no doubt the path, or seeming path, of the Sun in the celestial sphere; the Sun's diurnal orbit.

[599] Here, as often, *mere* is *absolute* or *downright*.

[600] The "golden couplets" are the two chicks of the dove; which, when first hatched, are covered with a *yellow* down; and in her patient tenderness the mother rarely leaves

His silence will sit drooping.
HAMLET. Hear you, sir;
    What is the reason that you use me thus?
    I loved you ever: but it is no matter;
    Let Hercules himself do what he may,
    The cat will mew and dog will have his day. [*Exit.*]
KING. I pray you, good Horatio, wait upon him.

    [*Exit* HORATIO.]

    [*To* LAERTES.] Strengthen your patience in our last night's
       speech;
    We'll put the matter to the present push.
    Good Gertrude, set some watch over your son.
    This grave shall have a living monument:
    An hour of quiet shortly shall we see;
    Till then, in patience our proceeding be. [*Exeunt.*]

SCENE II.

The Same. A Hall in the Castle.

[*Enter* HAMLET *and* HORATIO.]

HAMLET. So much for this, sir: now shall you see the other;
    You do remember all the circumstance?[601]
HORATIO. Remember it, my lord?
HAMLET. Sir, in my heart there was a kind of fighting,
    That would not let me sleep:[602] methought I lay
    Worse than the mutines in the bilboes.[603] Rashly,
    And praised be rashness for it—let us know,
    Our indiscretion sometimes serves us well,

---

the nest, till her little ones attain to some degree of dove-discretion.—*Disclose* was often used for *hatch.*

    [601] *Circumstance* means the *circumstantial account* given by Hamlet in his letter to Horatio.—*The other* refers to the further matter intimated in that letter: "I have words to speak in thine ear will make thee dumb."

    [602] Hamlet has from the first divined the King's purpose in sending him to England. Since the close of the interlude, Hamlet *knows* that the King did indeed murder his father, and he also knows that the King *suspects* him of knowing it. Hence, on shipboard, he naturally has a vague, general apprehension of mischief, and this fills him with nervous curiosity as to the particular shape of danger which he is to encounter.

    [603] The *bilboes* were bars of iron with fetters annexed to them, by which mutinous or disorderly sailors were linked together. To understand the allusion, it should be known that, as these fetters connected the legs of the offenders very closely together, their attempts to rest must be as fruitless as those of Hamlet, in whose mind *there was a kind of fighting that would not let him sleep.*—*Mutines* is for *mutineers.*

When our deep plots do pall;[604] and that should teach us
There's a divinity that shapes our ends,
Rough-hew them how we will.
HORATIO. That is most certain.
HAMLET. Up from my cabin,
My sea-gown scarf'd about me,[605] in the dark
Groped I to find out them; had my desire.
Finger'd their packet, and in fine withdrew
To mine own room again; making so bold,
My fears forgetting manners, to unseal
Their grand commission; where I found, Horatio,
Ah royal knavery! An exact command,
Larded with many several sorts of reasons
Importing Denmark's health and England's too,
With, ho! such bugs and goblins[606] in my life,
That, on the supervise, no leisure bated,[607]
No, not to stay the grinding of the axe,
My head should be struck off.
HORATIO. Is't possible?
HAMLET. Here's the commission: read it at more leisure.
But wilt thou hear me how I did proceed?
HORATIO. I beseech you.
HAMLET. Being thus be-netted round with villainies—
Ere I could make a prologue to my brains,
They had begun the play,[608]—I sat me down,
Devised a new commission, wrote it fair:
I once did hold it, as our statists do,
A baseness to write fair,[609] and labour'd much
How to forget that learning, but, sir, now
It did me yeoman's service.[610] Wilt thou know

---

[604] *Pall* is from the old French *palser*, to *fade* or *fall away*. So in *Antony and Cleopatra*, ii. 7: "I'll never follow thy *pall'd* fortunes more."—Note that all after *rashly*, down to Hamlet's next speech, is parenthetical.

[605] *Thrown*, or *gathered*, *loosely* about me.

[606] Such *bugbears* and *fantastic dangers growing out of* my life. The Poet has *bug* several times in that sense.—*Goblins* were a knavish sort of fairies, perhaps *ignes fatui*, and so belonged to the genus Humbug.

[607] The language is obscure, though the general sense is plain enough. I suspect *bated* is an instance of the passive form with the active sense; no leisure *abating* the speed; or the haste not being lessened by any pause.—*Supervise* is *looking over, perusal.*

[608] An allusion to the stage, where a play was commonly introduced by a prologue. Hamlet means that his thoughts were so fiery-footed as to start off in the play itself before he could get through the introduction.

[609] *Statist* is the old word for *statesman*. Blackstone says that "most of our great men of Shakespeare's time wrote very bad hands; their secretaries, very neat ones." It was accounted a mechanical and vulgar accomplishment to write a fair hand.

[610] In the days of archery, the English yeomanry, with their huge bows and long

The effect of what I wrote?

HORATIO. Ay, good my lord.

HAMLET. An earnest conjuration from the king,
  As England was his faithful tributary,
  As love between them like the palm might flourish,
  As peace should stiff her wheaten garland wear
  And stand a comma 'tween their amities,
  And many such-like ases of great charge,[611]
  That, on the view and knowing of these contents,
  Without debatement further, more or less,
  He should the bearers put to sudden death,
  Not shriving-time[612] allow'd.

HORATIO. How was this seal'd?

HAMLET. Why, even in that was heaven ordinant.
  I had my father's signet in my purse,
  Which was the model of that Danish seal;
  Folded the writ up in form of the other,
  Subscribed it, gave't the impression, placed it safely,
  The changeling never known. Now, the next day
  Was our sea-fight; and what to this was sequent
  Thou know'st already.

HORATIO. So Guildenstern and Rosencrantz go to't.

HAMLET. Why, man, they did make love to this employment;
  They are not near my conscience; their defeat
  Does by their own insinuation grow:
  'Tis dangerous when the baser nature comes
  Between the pass and fell incensed points
  Of mighty opposites.[613]

HORATIO. Why, what a king is this!

HAMLET. Does it not, think'st thee, stand me now upon?[614]
  He that hath kill'd my king and whored my mother,
  Popp'd in between the election and my hopes,
  Thrown out his angle for my proper life,
  And with such cozenage—is't not perfect conscience,
  To quit[615] him with this arm? and is't not to be damn'd,

---

arrows, were the most terrible fighters in Europe.

  [611] Of course "*ases*" refers to the use of *As* three times in the preceding lines. In Shakespeare's time *as* and *that* were often used interchangeably. So here; and, according to present usage, the second *As* and also the third should be *That.—Great charge* is *charged* with great *import.*

  [612] "*Shriving-time*" is time for confession and absolution.

  [613] When men of lower rank come between the thrusts and sword-points of great men engaged in fierce and mortal duel, or bent on fighting it out to the death.—Here, as usual in Shakespeare, *opposites* is *opponents.*

  [614] "It stands me upon" is an old phrase for "it is incumbent upon me," or, "it is my bounden duty."

To let this canker of our nature come
In further evil?[616]
HORATIO. It must be shortly known to him from England
What is the issue of the business there.
HAMLET. It will be short: the interim is mine;[617]
And a man's life's no more than to say 'One.'
But I am very sorry, good Horatio,
That to Laertes I forgot myself;
For, by the image of my cause, I see
The portraiture of his.[618] I'll court his favours.[619]
But, sure, the bravery of his grief did put me
Into a towering passion.
HORATIO. Peace! who comes here?

[*Enter* OSRIC.]

OSRIC. Your lordship is right welcome back to Denmark.
HAMLET. I humbly thank you, sir.—[*Aside to* HORATIO.] Dost
know this water-fly?[620]
HORATIO. [*Aside to* HAMLET.] No, my good lord.
HAMLET. [*Aside to* HORATIO.] Thy state is the more gracious; for
'tis a vice to know him. He hath much land, and fertile: let a beast
be lord of beasts, and his crib shall stand at the King's mess:[621] 'tis
a chough; but, as I say, spacious in the possession of dirt.
OSRIC. Sweet lord, if your lordship were at leisure, I should impart a
thing to you from his majesty.
HAMLET. I will receive it, sir, with all diligence of spirit. Put your
bonnet to his right use; 'tis for the head.
OSRIC. I thank your lordship, it is very hot.

---

[615] Here, as in many other places, to *quit* is to *requite*.

[616] "Is it not a damnable sin to let this *cancer* of humanity proceed further in mischief and villainy?" *Canker*, in one of its senses, means an eating, malignant sore, like a *cancer*.

[617] Hamlet justly looks forward to the coming of that news as the crisis of his task: it will give him a practicable twist on the King: he can then meet both him and the public with *justifying proof* of his guilt.

[618] Hamlet and Laertes have lost each his father, and both have perhaps lost equally in Ophelia; so that their cause of sorrow is much the same.

[619] Hamlet means "I'll solicit his *goodwill*"; the general meaning of *favours* in the Poet's time.

[620] In *Troilus and Cressida*, v. 1, Thersites says of Patroclus, "How the poor world is pestered with such *water-flies*, diminutives of Nature!" As Johnson says, "A water-fly skips up and down upon the surface of the water without any apparent purpose or reason, and is thence the proper emblem of a busy trifler."

[621] This is meant as a sarcastic stroke at the King for keeping such a finical sap-head near his person. Let even a biped puppy be rich, the lord or owner of large herds of cattle, and he shall be the King's bosom friend, and feed at his table.—*Chough* is a bird of the jackdaw sort; and Osric is aptly so called because he chatters euphuistic jargon *by rote*.

HAMLET. No, believe me, 'tis very cold; the wind is northerly.

OSRIC. It is indifferent cold, my lord, indeed.

HAMLET. But yet methinks it is very sultry and hot for my
complexion.

OSRIC. Exceedingly, my lord; it is very sultry, as 'twere—I cannot tell
how. But, my lord, his majesty bade me signify to you that he has
laid a great wager on your head: sir, this is the matter—

HAMLET. I beseech you, remember.[622]

[HAMLET *moves him to put on his hat.*]

OSRIC. Nay, good my lord; for mine ease, in good faith. Sir, here is
newly come to court Laertes; believe me, an absolute gentleman,
full of most excellent differences,[623] of very soft society and great
showing: indeed, to speak feelingly of him, he is the card or
calendar of gentry, for you shall find in him the continent of what
part a gentleman would see.

HAMLET. Sir, his definement suffers no perdition in you;[624] though, I
know, to divide him inventorially would dizzy the arithmetic of
memory,[625] and yet but yaw neither, in respect of his quick sail.[626]
But, in the verity of extolment, I take him to be a soul of great
article; and his infusion of such dearth and rareness, as, to make
true diction of him, his semblable is his mirror; and who else
would trace him, his umbrage,[627] nothing more.

OSRIC. Your lordship speaks most infallibly of him.

---

[622] When one takes off his hat in courtesy to another, courtesy requires that he
should presently put it on again, and not stand with it in his hand. So here the full
meaning is, "Remember your courtesy, and put on your hat."

[623] In the affected phrase-making of this euphuist, *excellent differences* probably
means *distinctive excellences.*

[624] "He suffers no *loss* in your *description* of him."

[625] "To *distinguish* all his good parts, and make a schedule or *inventory* of them,
would be too much for the most mathematical head."—The word *yaw* occurs as a
substantive in Massinger's *Very Woman;* "O, *the yaws* that she will make! Look to your
stern, dear mistress, and steer right." Where Gifford notes, "A *yaw* is that unsteady
motion which a ship makes in a great swell, when, in steering, she inclines to the right or
left of her course." In the text, *yaw* is a verb, and in the same construction with *dizzy;*
"and yet would do nothing but *reel hither and thither.*"

[626] *In respect of* is equivalent to *in comparison with.* So that the sense of the passage
comes thus: "To discriminate the good parts of Laertes, and make a full catalogue of
them, would dizzy the head of an arithmetician, and yet would be but a slow and
staggering process, *compared to* his swift sailing." Hamlet is running Osric's
hyperbolical euphuism into the ground, and is purposely obscure, in order to bewilder the
poor fop.

[627] To *trace* is to *track,* or *keep pace* with. *Umbrage,* from the Latin *umbra,* is
shadow. So that the meaning here is, "The only resemblance to him is in his mirror; and
nothing but his shadow can keep up with him."

HAMLET. The concernancy,[628] sir? why do we wrap the gentleman in our more rawer breath?

OSRIC. Sir?

HORATIO. Is't not possible to understand in another tongue?[629] You will do't, sir, really.

HAMLET. What imports the nomination of this gentleman?

OSRIC. Of Laertes?

HORATIO. [*Aside to* HAMLET.] His purse is empty already; all's golden words are spent.

HAMLET. Of him, sir.

OSRIC. I know you are not ignorant—

HAMLET. I would you did, sir; yet, in faith, if you did, it would not much approve me. Well, sir?

OSRIC. You are not ignorant of what excellence Laertes is—

HAMLET. I dare not confess that, lest I should compare with him in excellence; but, to know a man well, were to know himself.[630]

OSRIC. I mean, sir, for his weapon; but in the imputation laid on him by them, in his meed he's unfellow'd.[631]

HAMLET. What's his weapon?

OSRIC. Rapier and dagger.

HAMLET. That's two of his weapons: but, well.

OSRIC. The King, sir, hath wagered with him six Barbary horses: against the which he has imponed,[632] as I take it, six French rapiers and poniards, with their assigns, as girdle, hangers, and so: three of the carriages, in faith, are very dear to fancy, very responsive to the hilts, most delicate carriages, and of very liberal conceit.

HAMLET. What call you the carriages?

HORATIO. [*Aside to* HAMLET.] I knew you must be edified by the margent[633] ere you had done.

---

[628] That is, "How does this concern us?"

[629] Horatio means to imply that what with Osric's euphuism, and what with Hamlet's catching of Osric's style, they are not speaking in a tongue that can be understood; and he hints that they try *another* tongue, that is, the common one.

[630] The meaning is, that he will not claim to appreciate the excellence of Laertes, as this would imply equal excellence in himself; on the principle that a man cannot understand that which exceeds his own measure. Hamlet goes into these subtilties on purpose to maze Osric.—The words, "*but* to know," mean "*only* to know." Ignorance or oversight of this has sometimes caused the text to be thought corrupt.

[631] *Unfellow'd* is *unequalled. Fellow* for *equal* is very frequent.—*Meed* for *merit*; also a frequent usage.—*Imputation*, also, for *reputation*. So in *Troilus and Cressida*, i. 3: "Our *imputation* shall be oddly poised in this wild action." All used here, however, with euphuistic affectation.

[632] *Imponed* is probably meant as an Osrican form of *impawned*. To *impawn* is to *put in pledge*, to *stake* or *wager*.

[633] "I knew you *would have to be* instructed by a *marginal commentary*." The allusion is to the printing of comments in the margin of books. So in *Romeo and* Juliet, i. 3:

OSRIC. The carriages, sir, are the hangers.

HAMLET. The phrase would be more germane[634] to the matter, if we could carry cannon by our sides: I would it might be hangers till then. But, on: six Barbary horses against six French swords, their assigns, and three liberal-conceited carriages; that's the French bet against the Danish. Why is this 'imponed,' as you call it?

OSRIC. The king, sir, hath laid, that in a dozen passes between yourself and him, he shall not exceed you three hits: he hath laid on twelve for nine; and it would come to immediate trial, if your lordship would vouchsafe the answer.[635]

HAMLET. How if I answer 'no'?

OSRIC. I mean, my lord, the opposition of your person in trial.

HAMLET. Sir, I will walk here in the hall: if it please his majesty, 'tis the breathing time[636] of day with me; let the foils be brought, the gentleman willing, and the king hold his purpose, I will win for him an I can; if not, I will gain nothing but my shame and the odd hits.

OSRIC. Shall I re-deliver you e'en so?

HAMLET. To this effect, sir; after what flourish your nature will.

OSRIC. I commend my duty to your lordship.

HAMLET. Yours, yours. [*Exit* OSRIC.] He does well to commend it himself; there are no tongues else for's turn.

HORATIO. This lapwing runs away with the shell on his head.[637]

HAMLET. He did comply with his dug,[638] before he sucked it. Thus has he—and many more of the same bevy that I know the dressy age dotes on—only got the tune of the time and outward habit of encounter; a kind of yeasty collection,[639] which carries them through and through the most fond and winnowed opinions;[640] and do but blow them to their trial, the bubbles are out.

And what obscured in this fair volume lies,
Find written in the margent of his eyes.

[634] *Germane* is *kindred* or *akin*; hence, *appropriate*.

[635] That is, vouchsafe to *accept the proposition*. Hamlet chooses to take it in another sense, because he likes to quiz Osric.

[636] "The *breathing-time*" is the time for *exercise*. The use of to *breathe* for to *exercise* occurs repeatedly in Shakespeare. It was common.

[637] Meaning that Osric is a raw, unfledged, foolish fellow. It was a comparison for a forward fool. So in Meres's *Wits Treasury*, 1598: "As the lapwing runneth away with the shell on her head, as soon as she is hatched."

[638] *Comply* is used in the same sense here as in note 281. In Fulwel's *Art of Flatterie*, 1579, the same idea occurs: "The very sucking babes hath a kind of adulation towards their nurses for the dug."

[639] *Yesty* is *frothy*. A *gathering* of mental and lingual froth.

[640] Here, *fond* is *affected*. The passage is well explained in the Clarendon edition: "Osric, and others like him, are compared to the chaff which mounts higher than the sifted wheat, and to the bubbles which rise to the surface through the deeper water."

[*Enter a* LORD.]

LORD. My lord, his majesty commended him to you by young Osric, who brings back to him that you attend him in the hall: he sends to know if your pleasure hold to play with Laertes, or that you will take longer time.

HAMLET. I am constant to my purpose; they follow the king's pleasure: if his fitness speaks, mine is ready; now or whensoever, provided I be so able as now.

LORD. The king and queen and all are coming down.

HAMLET. In happy time.[641]

LORD. The queen desires you to use some gentle entertainment to Laertes before you fall to play.

HAMLET. She well instructs me. [*Exit* LORD.]

HORATIO. You will lose this wager, my lord.

HAMLET. I do not think so: since he went into France, I have been in continual practise: I shall win at the odds. But thou wouldst not think how ill all's here about my heart: but it is no matter.

HORATIO. Nay, good my lord—

HAMLET. It is but foolery; but it is such a kind of gain-giving,[642] as would perhaps trouble a woman.

HORATIO. If your mind dislike any thing, obey it: I will forestall their repair hither, and say you are not fit.

HAMLET. Not a whit, we defy[643] augury: there's a special providence in the fall of a sparrow. If it be now, 'tis not to come; if it be not to come, it will be now; if it be not now, yet it will come: the readiness is all: since no man has aught of what he leaves, what is't to leave betimes?[644]

[*Enter the* KING, *the* QUEEN, LAERTES, LORDS, OSRIC, *and* ATTENDANTS *with foils, &c.*]

KING. Come, Hamlet, come, and take this hand from me.

[*The* KING *puts* LAERTES's *hand into* HAMLET's.]

HAMLET. Give me your pardon, sir: I've done you wrong;

---

[641] That is, in *fitting* time; like the French *a la bonne heure.*

[642] *Gain-giving* probably means *misgiving*; formed in the same way as *gainsay* and *gainstrive.*

[643] To *defy*, here, is to *renounce* or *disclaim.* Often so.

[644] Johnson interprets the passage thus: "Since *no man knows aught* of the state which *he leaves*; since he cannot judge what other years may produce; why should we be afraid of *leaving* life betimes?"

But pardon't, as you are a gentleman.
This presence knows,
And you must needs have heard, how I am punish'd
With sore distraction. What I have done,
That might your nature, honour and exception
Roughly awake, I here proclaim was madness.
Was't Hamlet wrong'd Laertes? Never Hamlet.
If Hamlet from himself be ta'en away,
And when he's not himself does wrong Laertes,
Then Hamlet does it not, Hamlet denies it.
Who does it, then? His madness: if't be so,
Hamlet is of the faction that is wrong'd;
His madness is poor Hamlet's enemy.
Sir, in this audience,
Let my disclaiming from a purposed evil
Free me so far in your most generous thoughts,
That I have shot mine arrow o'er the house,
And hurt my brother.

LAERTES. I am satisfied in nature,
Whose motive, in this case, should stir me most
To my revenge: but in my terms of honour
I stand aloof; and will no reconcilement,
Till by some elder masters, of known honour,
I have a voice and precedent of peace,[645]
To keep my name ungor'd—but till that time,
I do receive your offer'd love like love,
And will not wrong it.

HAMLET. I embrace it freely;
And will this brother's wager frankly play.
Give us the foils. Come on.

LAERTES. Come, one for me.

HAMLET. I'll be your foil, Laertes:[646] in mine ignorance
Your skill shall, like a star i' the darkest night,
Stick fiery off indeed.

LAERTES. You mock me, sir.

HAMLET. No, by this hand.

---

[645] The meaning probably is, "till some experts in the code of honour give me the warrant of custom and usage for standing on peaceful terms with you." Laertes thinks, or pretends to think, that the laws of honour require him to insist on a stern vindication of his manhood. Hamlet has before spoken of Laertes as "a very noble youth." In this part of the scene, he has his faculties keenly on the alert against Claudius; but it were a sin in him even to suspect Laertes of any thing so unfathomably base as the treachery now on foot.

[646] Hamlet plays on the word *foil*; which here has the sense of *contrast*, or that which *sets off* a thing, and makes it show to advantage; as a dark night sets off a star, "when only one is shining in the sky."

KING. Give them the foils, young Osric. Cousin Hamlet,
You know the wager?
HAMLET. Very well, my lord
Your grace hath laid the odds o' the weaker side.[647]
KING. I do not fear it; I have seen you both:
But since he is better'd, we have therefore odds.[648]
LAERTES. This is too heavy, let me see another.
HAMLET. This likes me well. These foils have all a length?

[*They prepare to play.*]

OSRIC. Ay, my good lord.
KING. Set me the stoops of wine upon that table.—
If Hamlet give the first or second hit,
Or quit[649] in answer of the third exchange,
Let all the battlements their ordnance fire:
The king shall drink to Hamlet's better breath;
And in the cup an union[650] shall he throw,
Richer than that which four successive kings
In Denmark's crown have worn. Give me the cups;
And let the kettle to the trumpet speak,
The trumpet to the cannoneer without,
The cannons to the heavens, the heavens to earth,
'Now the king dunks to Hamlet.' Come, begin:
And you, the judges,[651] bear a wary eye.
HAMLET. Come on, sir.
LAERTES. Come, my lord. [*They play.*]
HAMLET. One.
LAERTES. No.
HAMLET. Judgment.
OSRIC. A hit, a very palpable hit.
LAERTES. Well; again.
KING. Stay; give me drink. Hamlet, this pearl is thine;
Here's to thy health.

---

[647] The *odds* here referred to is the value of the stakes, the King having wagered six Barbary horses against a few rapiers, poniards, &c,; which was about as twenty to one.

[648] Here the reference is to the *three odd* hits in Hamlet's favour, the numbers being nine and twelve. The King affects to regard this as a fair offset for Laertes's improved skill in the handling of his weapon.

[649] *Quit*, again, for *requite*, or *retaliate*.

[650] *Union* was a name for the largest and finest pearls, such as were worn in crowns and coronets. So in Florio's *Italian Dictionary*, 1598: "Also a faire, great, orient pearle, called an *union*." A rich gem thus put into a cup of wine was meant as present to the drinker of the wine. Of course the *union* in this case was a preparation of poison.

[651] These *judges* were the umpires appointed beforehand, with Osric at their head, to decide in case of any dispute arising between the fencers.

[*Trumpets sound, and cannon shot off within.*]

    Give him the cup.

HAMLET. I'll play this bout first; set it by awhile. Come.—[*They play.*] Another hit; what say you?

LAERTES. A touch, a touch, I do confess.

KING. Our son shall win.

QUEEN. He's hot, and scant of breath.

    Here, Hamlet, take my napkin,[652] rub thy brows;

    The queen carouses to thy fortune, Hamlet.

HAMLET. Good madam![653]

KING. Gertrude, do not drink.

QUEEN. I will, my lord; I pray you, pardon me. [*Drinks.*]

KING. [*Aside.*] It is the poison'd cup: it is too late.

HAMLET. I dare not drink yet, madam; by and by.[654]

QUEEN. Come, let me wipe thy face.

LAERTES. My lord, I'll hit him now.

KING. I do not think't.

LAERTES. [*Aside.*] And yet 'tis almost 'gainst my conscience.

HAMLET. Come, for the third, Laertes: you but dally;

    I pray you, pass with your best violence;

    I am afeard you make a wanton of me.[655]

LAERTES. Say you so? come on. [*They play.*]

OSRIC. Nothing, neither way.

LAERTES. Have at you now!

    [LAERTES *wounds* HAMLET; *then in scuffling, they change foils, and* HAMLET *wounds* LAERTES.[656]]

---

[652] *Napkin* was continually used for *handkerchief.*

[653] This exclamation is probably meant to hint that Hamlet suspects, or more than suspects, the contents of that cup. The same appears more clearly just after in "I dare not drink yet."

[654] Hamlet now sees, or judges, that his time has come: the playing done, he will attend to that cup, and *invite Claudius to drink it.* Such is evidently his purpose.

[655] To make a wanton of a man, as the phrase is here used, is to treat him as a child, to avoid playing your best with him, or rather to play the game into his hands.—This is a quiet, but very significant stroke of delineation. Laertes is not playing his best, and it is the conscience of what is at the point of his foil that keeps him from doing so; and the effects are perceptible to Hamlet, though he dreams not of the reason.

[656] Up to this moment Hamlet has not put forth his strength; he has been *merely* playing; now, on being unexpectedly pierced, he is instantly stung into fiery action; and he is a terrible man with the sword, when his blood is up.—The exchanging of foils takes place well in Mr. Edwin Booth's ordering of the matter on the stage. There Hamlet, in a rapture of energy and adroitness, strikes the foil out of Laertes's hand, picks it up, and throws down his own, which is presently picked up by Laertes.

KING. Part them; they are incensed.

HAMLET. Nay, come, again. [*The* QUEEN *falls.*]

OSRIC. Look to the queen there, ho!

HORATIO. They bleed on both sides. How is it, my lord?

OSRIC. How is't, Laertes?

LAERTES. Why, as a woodcock to mine own springe, Osric;
    I am justly kill'd with mine own treachery.

HAMLET. How does the queen?

KING. She swoons to see them bleed.

QUEEN. No, no, the drink, the drink! O my dear Hamlet!
    The drink, the drink! I am poison'd. [*Dies.*]

HAMLET. O villainy! Ho! let the door be lock'd.
    Treachery! Seek it out.

LAERTES. It is here, Hamlet: Hamlet, thou art slain;
    No medicine in the world can do thee good;
    In thee there is not half an hour of life;
    The treacherous instrument is in thy hand,
    Unbated and envenom'd. Thy foul practice
    Hath turn'd itself on me lo, here I lie,
    Never to rise again: thy mother's poison'd:
    I can no more: the king, the king's to blame.

HAMLET. The point!—envenom'd too!
    Then, venom, to thy work. [*Stabs the* KING.]

ALL. Treason! treason!

KING. O, yet defend me, friends; I am but hurt.

HAMLET. Here, thou incestuous, murderous, damned Dane,
    Drink off this potion. Is thy union here?
    Follow my mother. [*The* KING *dies.*[657]]

LAERTES. He is justly served;
    It is a poison temper'd by himself.
    Exchange forgiveness with me, noble Hamlet:
    Mine and my father's death come not upon thee,
    Nor thine on me. [*Dies.*[658]]

HAMLET. Heaven make thee free of it! I follow thee.
    I am dead, Horatio. Wretched queen, adieu!
    You that look pale and tremble at this chance,
    That are but mutes or audience to this act,
    Had I but time—as this fell sergeant,[659] death,
    Is strict in his arrest—O, I could tell you—

---

[657] Of course the King dies of the wound,—dies without drinking the poison. Hamlet, instantly seeing the way clear for the avenging stroke, and having a free thrust at Claudius, can hardly be supposed to leave any thing for poison to do.

[658] Laertes also dies of the *wound*, not of the *venom*.

[659] *Sergeant* was the title of a sheriff's officer, whose business it was to make arrests and execute warrants.

But let it be. Horatio, I am dead;
Thou livest; report me and my cause aright
To the unsatisfied.
HORATIO. Never believe it:
I am more an antique Roman than a Dane:
Here's yet some liquor left.
HAMLET. As th'art a man,
Give me the cup: let go; by heaven, I'll ha't.
O good Horatio, what a wounded name,
Things standing thus unknown, shall live behind me!
If thou didst ever hold me in thy heart
Absent thee from felicity awhile,
And in this harsh world draw thy breath in pain,
To tell my story.—[*March afar off, and shot within.*]
        What warlike noise is this?
OSRIC. Young Fortinbras, with conquest come from Poland,
To the ambassadors of England gives
This warlike volley.
HAMLET. O, I die, Horatio;
The potent poison quite o'er-crows[660] my spirit:
I cannot live to hear the news from England;
But I do prophesy the election lights
On Fortinbras: he has my dying voice;
So tell him, with the occurrents, more and less,
Which have solicited[661]—[*Dies.*]
HORATIO. The rest is silence.
Now cracks a noble heart. Good night sweet prince:
And flights of angels sing thee to thy rest!
Why does the drum come hither? [*March within.*]

[*Enter* FORTINBRAS, *the* ENGLISH AMBASSADORS, *and others.*]

FORTINBRAS. Where is this sight?
HORATIO. What is it ye would see?
If aught of woe or wonder, cease your search.
FORTINBRAS. This quarry cries on[662] havoc. O proud death,

---

[660] To *overcrow* is to *overcome*, to *subdue*. The word was borrowed from the cock-pit; the victorious cock crowing in triumph over the vanquished.

[661] *Occurrents* was much used in the Poet's time for *events* or *occurrences.*—*Solicited* is *prompted* or *excited*; as "this supernatural *soliciting*" in Macbeth.—"*More and less*" is *greater* and *smaller*; a common usage with the old writers.

[662] *Quarry*, a term of the chase, was used for a *heap of dead game*. To *cry on*, as before noted, is to *exclaim*, or *cry out, against*. *Havoc* here means *indiscriminate slaughter*. To shout *havoc*! in a battle, was a signal for giving no quarter to the enemy.

What feast is toward[663] in thine eternal cell,
That thou so many princes at a shot
So bloodily hast struck?
FIRST AMBASSADOR. The sight is dismal;
And our affairs from England come too late:
The ears are senseless that should give us hearing,
To tell him his commandment is fulfill'd,
That Rosencrantz and Guildenstern are dead:
Where should we have our thanks?
HORATIO. Not from his mouth,
Had it the ability of life to thank you:
He never gave commandment for their death.
But since, so jump upon this bloody question,
You from the Polack wars, and you from England,
Are here arrived give order that these bodies
High on a stage be placed to the view;
And let me speak to the yet unknowing world
How these things came about: so shall you hear
Of carnal,[664] bloody, and unnatural acts,
Of accidental judgments, casual slaughters,
Of deaths put on by cunning and forced cause,[665]
And, in this upshot, purposes mistook
Fall'n on the inventors' reads: all this can I
Truly deliver.
FORTINBRAS. Let us haste to hear it,
And call the noblest to the audience.
For me, with sorrow I embrace my fortune:
I have some rights of memory[666] in this kingdom,
Which now to claim my vantage doth invite me.
HORATIO. Of that I shall have also cause to speak,
And from his mouth whose voice will draw on more;[667]
But let this same be presently perform'd,
Even while men's minds are wild; lest more mischance
On plots and errors, happen.
FORTINBRAS. Let four captains
Bear Hamlet, like a soldier, to the stage;

---

[663] *Toward*, again, *fox forthcoming*, or *at hand.*

[664] *Carnal*, here, probably means *sanguinary*, *cruel*, or *inhuman*; referring to the murder of Hamlet's father.

[665] The phrase *put on* here means *instigated* or *set on foot*. *Cunning*, refers, apparently, to Hamlet's action touching "the packet," and *forced cause*, to the "compelling occasion" which moved him to that piece of practice.

[666] *Rights of memory* appears to mean rights founded in prescription or the order of inheritance.

[667] Whose vote will induce others to vote the same way. Horatio refers to Hamlet saying of Fortinbras, "he has my dying voice."

For he was likely, had he been put on,
To have proved most royally: and, for his passage,
The soldiers' music and the rites of war
Speak loudly for him.
Take up the bodies: such a sight as this
Becomes the field, but here shows much amiss.
Go, bid the soldiers shoot.

[*A dead march. Exeunt, bearing off the dead bodies; after which a peal of ordnance is shot off.*]

THE END